COAST OF SWEDEN

© Bokförlaget Max Ström 2007
Text: Tommy Hammarström
Translation: Greg McIvor with
Kevin Billinghurst and Fenela Childs
Editor: Katarina Trodden
Picture research: Cenneth Sparby
Design: Patric Leo
Layout: Amelie Stenbeck-Ramel
Printing: Fälth & Hässler, Värnamo, Sweden 2008
Second impression
ISBN 978-91-7126-100-7

COAST OF SWEDEN

TEXT TOMMY HAMMARSTRÖM

*Photographers Tore Hagman, Jeppe Wikström, Lars Bygdemark, Malcolm Hanes, Magnus Rietz,
L-G Abrahamsson, Martin Borg, Bengt S Eriksson, Jonas Forsberg, Hans Geijer,
Claes Grundsten, Sven Halling, Bengt Hedberg, Christer Häggström, Pär Jacobsson, Ove Källström,
Peter Lilja, Kjell Ljungström, Roine Magnusson, Sven Persson, Jan Rietz, Klas Rune,
Håkan Sandbring, Hasse Schröder, Hans Strand, Mikael Svensson, Jan Töve, Jörgen Wiklund*

Bokförlaget Max Ström

CONTENTS

Introduction 7

West Coast 12

South Coast 60

East Coast 100

Öland and Gotland 136

Stockholm Archipelago 168

North Coast 210

Winter Coast 248

WHAT DRAWS US TO THE SEA?

The sea is where freedom is, in the words of the twentieth century Swedish poet and singer Evert Taube. But that is not the whole answer. Our passion for the ocean runs more deeply; it is embedded in our souls and lies at the heart of the human psyche. We are drawn to the sea because it supports our very existence.

The first humans who came to Sweden after the Ice Age explored the coastline by boat and on foot, subsisting on a diet of fish, seal meat and birds' eggs. On log boats and rafts they sailed over the rocks of Bohuslän, through Östergötland, Uppland and far north to Norrland in the same type of hewn wooden boats we find depicted on Cretan pottery fragments.

Though omnivorous by nature, man is from an evolutionary perspective best adapted to a sea-based diet of fish, shellfish, seal meat and seafowl. When we say we are drawn to the coast and its islands – to the sea – it does indeed reflect a yearning for freedom: the freedom that comes from ready access to life's essentials, food and transport.

Of course, people no longer think of it in those terms. For us, the archipelago is where we go to sunbathe, swim and maybe, just maybe, to try and catch a pike to bake and serve with butter and horseradish.

We take to our boats, not for transport but simply to get away from it all and experience that wonderful feeling of independence. The sea has become a place of leisure and rest. Coastal communities no longer rely on fishing but on tourism. And when we talk about freedom, we mean freedom from necessity. We no longer realise that we love the sea because it offers us livelihoods and survival. But love it we do, as much as we ever did.

Sweden has a very long coast. From the Norwegian border in the northwest to the Finnish border in the far north-east, it is roughly seven thousand kilometres long. What makes it so special is its unique island archipelagos. The entire coast, aside from southern Halland and northeast Skåne, is dotted with numerous islands, islets and skerries. The official number is 221,800, though this count also includes the multitude of islands on inland lakes. If you only count sea islands, the figure is closer to 70,000. No other country in the world, bar Finland, has such a vast coastal archipelago.

The archipelago is both an old and a new world. Virtually all the islands are of granite and gneiss bedrock aged between one and two billion years old. Such ancient stone is almost always covered by younger, sedimentary rock – but not in Sweden. Geologists from around the world visit the country to study the formations.

Though made of ancient rock, the islands and skerries have only been above sea level for ten thousand years. They and the surrounding coast-line were formed by the land uplift caused when the glaciers retreated at the end of the last Ice Age. The process is still ongoing; land eleva-tion adds one hundred hectares to the Kvarken archipelago in northern Sweden each year.

Scoured by ice and smoothed by the sea, the gentle, flat slopes and con-tours of archipelago islands are perfect for sunbathers and swimmers, and the crevices in between provide shelter when the wind bites. For many, the low-lying islands are the quintessence of Swedish coastal life.

My first memories of an island summer are from Södra Finnö in the Sankt Anna archipelago, south-west of Norrköping. It was the summer of 1949. I was three years old and spent my time paddling in the shallow, crystal-clear water of the tiny inlet beside the house where we rented a garret from a rich lady from Ämtö, another island farther to the north. I remember so clearly the inviting, white sand and daring to sit on it while I explored the shallows. I remember, too, trying to sidestep the dark pat-ches of seaweed. "Don't worry, they're not dangerous," my father would tell me, demonstrating how to pop the kelp bubbles with a little smack of the hand.

The sand, the clear water and the seaweed – my first archipelago memories. And the granite rock, of course, which jutted up everywhere and was caked in white peat moss apart from down at the water's edge. Not to mention all the flowers: wild pansies in between the rocks and les-ser butterfly-orchids under the oak trees.

We had a boat with a cabin and hot bulb engine. Dad would kick-start the motor and I was always scared the flywheel would jump backwards. It was a nasty machine; you had to use a blow-torch to ignite the hot-bulb and I was not allowed on board until the motor was firing properly. From a distance, the gentle throbbing of these craft was a familiar and com-forting sound and one I will never forget. These days, the high-pitched whine of petrol engines has taken over.

Once we towed a sailing boat over Flisdjupet. The wind was gale-force, whipping in from the open sea to the south-east. The boat was an A22, the most stylish yacht ever made, and I remember how happy and relieved the crew were when we found shelter from the wind behind Flisö.

We were among the first summer visitors to Finnö, where we stayed in our spartanly furnished room high up in the house. The rent included water from a well but little else, not even rights to fish in the sea. I remember the butterflies in my stomach every time my father cast his line and poached a pike. The fishing was amazing; we never failed to catch a pike or two. Once we even managed to sneak out with an eel line baited with a hundred hooks, I've no idea how, and fished up a rich catch of eel and perch. What a feast we had!

A few years ago I returned to Finnö. The house where we rented our room was still there, just as I remembered it, but the inlet where we used to swim was gone, closed up by land uplift and the clump of sedges now growing in the nutrient-rich water. The crystal-clear water was not clear any more, and the forests of kelp had been crowded out by green, fibrous algae.

All the old farmhouses have been converted into summer homes, while enormous plastic boats with satellite navigation systems are moored by the fishing huts. These days, you are allowed to fish, but the pickings are few. Numbers of pike and perch have fallen sharply and the eel is currently threatened with extinction. The rocks are still there, along with the pansies and orchids and the tall ash tree down by the gate. But these are new times now, and though I long to go back again, the nostalgia hurts.

This book tells the story of the Swedish coast and its sea and islands, its beaches and bays, and its old fishermen's haunts and summer places. It starts on the West Coast, at Nordkoster's newly renovated lighthouse, and continues down through the provinces of Bohuslän and Halland to Varberg, where the granite islands of the West Coast give way to the flat, dune landscape of the South Coast.

With its bare rocks and densely populated islands, windswept hamlets and summertime hustle and bustle, the West Coast is a mixture of the barren and the bountiful. Where once the giant shoals of herring made it rich, it is now affluent from tourism.

From the fishing village of Träslövsläge in Halland to Åhus on Skåne's east coast, the shoreline has no archipelagos or islands to protect it from the sea. There is a more continental feel, rather like the Danish and North German coasts, and like them characterised by flat beaches and coastal meadows. Beach huts dot the seashore and the old fishing villages have been converted into summer resorts.

At Listerlandet in Blekinge province the archipelago rises again from the sea, snaking northwards all the way to the Gulf of Bothnia. The East Coast encompasses the archipelagos of Blekinge, Småland, Östergötland and Sörmland and changes in character along its length. From the leafy islands and stately oaks of Blekinge it progresses to the Cambrian sediment beaches and islands of Kalmar Sound and on to the myriad islands and skerries of Misterhult, the fjord-like bays of the Västervik and Tjust archipelagos and the stony, raised islands of Gryt. Next come the large, lush islands of the Sankt Anna archipelago and, finally, the archipelagos of Oxelösund, Nyköping and Trosa.

Öland and Gotland are in a category of their own: two large islands with a unique geology, their own history and a distinctive flora and fauna. Steep cliffs and strange, mystical shapes and forms are sculpted in the calcareous, sedimentary rock. Livestock grazing keeps the vegetation on the heaths and limestone plains so short that soil erosion is a major problem, though the abundance of flowers and birdlife attracts botanists and ornithologists from all over Sweden and beyond.

The Stockholm archipelago's closeness to the capital has left a heavy imprint on its islands. It is the largest and widest of the archipelagos and boasts more islands than any other. More feted and written about than any of Sweden's other island hinterlands, it occupies a special place in the national soul.

The long Norrland Coast runs from the Bay of Gävle to the Gulf of Bothnia and is well forested, with a mostly narrow string of islands. Industrial forestry has disfigured many areas, but with time the scars heal and many parts are now recovering. Untouched areas can still be found, especially along the Virgin Coast of Gästrikland and Hälsingland provinces. The High Coast of Ångermanland province, with its lofty hills that are still rising from the sea, is a World Heritage site.

As you will soon discover, the Swedish coast is a magnificent, captivating and picturesque world. But wherein lies the beauty? Do we see beauty because that is what we are looking for? I believe so. We are drawn to the sea, the coast and the archipelago, and in our longing to be there lies the beauty.

WEST COAST

This is Sweden's gateway to the ocean. For centuries it was the richest coast, made prosperous by shipping, fishing and quarrying. Today, the islands between Koster and Varberg are a paradise for everyone who yearns for the open horizon.

The rocks rise from the sea, first as reefs, then as slabs and dark granite ridges. Closer to shore their bulging, undulating forms plunge deep into the clear water.

It is a barren, inhospitable landscape that greets incoming sailors from the Skagerrak and the Kattegatt. The botanist and zoologist Carl Linnaeus called it a world of "sheer drops", commenting in 1746 that the treeless and bare rocks were a poor environment for plants. "Were any plant to germinate or take root in the crevices it would, as soon as it were fully grown, be baked dry by the sun or eaten by animals."

So strange, then, to see the tightly packed houses that cling to the rocksides in places like Fjällbacka, Smögen, Gullholmen and Åstol. These colourful, higgledy-piggledy villages are at odds with the infertile ground on which they stand. A rich mixture of shapes and sizes, they owe their existence not to the land but to the sea's hidden treasures – the shoals of herring and cod and the prawns and lobsters.

The West Coast's heritage is inextricably tied to fishing, especially for herring. From the Stone Age onwards, its history was dictated by the so-called herring periods – enigmatic events that occurred roughly once a century, but were impossible to predict and never fully understood.

Out of the blue, the herring would appear in giant shoals offshore and people would rush to the coast to take advantage of the harvest. The bounty would last for forty or fifty years before disappearing as abruptly as it had begun. The fish would then be gone for sixty or seventy years before reappearing in vast numbers again.

First recorded during the Viking era, great herring periods were noted in 1195–1250, 1307–1362, 1419–1474, 1556–1587, 1660–1680, 1749–1808 and 1877–1906. Since then, however, all has been quiet on the herring front and in all likelihood we will not witness a great herring run again. Why? Because the stocks are farther offshore nowadays, and are fished long before they get the chance to head for the coast en masse.

The arrival of motorised fishing boats enabled fishermen to venture farther from the coast than before. In doing so, they realised that herring shoals are more or less ever-present in the waters of the Skagerrak and Kattegatt. The herring periods were an inshore event, between which

Evening sun falls on red granite in Fjällbacka, a favourite tourist destination in northern Bohuslän and home to a sizeable lobster fleet. The red warehouses in the harbour were built at the peak of the herring era in the eighteenth century (p. 12).

Fishing shacks on a still summer evening. Sydkoster, where some 200 permanent residents are joined by up to 8,000 overnight visitors during the summer (pp. 14–15).

Marstrand, a west coast hub for sailors. During the sixteenth century herring fishing era, Marstrand – then Danish – boomed. But the town fell on hard times as overfishing took its toll. By 1645, Marstrand was Swedish, and at the end of the eighteenth century it was declared *porto franco*, a free port (previous pages).

Hållö, near Smögen. Primary rock polished by inland ice and frugally decorated by lichen. There has been a lighthouse on Hållö since 1842.

19

the fish simply relocated to deeper waters farther out. Nowadays, we can simply follow the shoals in our modern boats rather than have to wait for them to reappear closer to home. So by the time the herring in the old days would have been ready to invade the coastline, they have already been caught, salted, pickled or ground into animal feed.

Back in the 1960s, author Carl Fries travelled to Bohuslän, the West Coast's northernmost province and heart of the old herring fishing industry, and predicted a new herring period was in the offing. "Sixty years have passed since the last great herring invasion in Bohuslän's fjords," he wrote. "Going back through the centuries, there were a minimum of fifty-seven and a maximum of eighty-two years between these times of plenty. In the winter of 1964–1965 some strange catches of large herring were made. Are these the advance guard from the north? There's excitement in the air."

But the growth of industrial fishing ensured that Fries's prediction never came to pass. The early 1960s saw the advent of highly efficient purse-seine fishing, whereby large boats pulled huge nets up to five hundred metres long and one hundred and sixty metres deep up and down the North Sea, dragging up enough herring and mackerel to make their holds bulge. The catches were so big that boats would on occasion become so overloaded as to capsize and sink.

In less than fifteen years, herring stocks were on the verge of collapse. A total ban on herring fishing was introduced in Icelandic waters and the North Sea from 1978 to 1983. It came in time to save the North Sea stocks but not those in Iceland, which have yet to recover thirty years on.

Since then, the fishing industry has been plagued by over-capacity and forced to grapple with the bureaucracy of quotas, economic zones and other technicalities. What was once the mainstay of West Coast life is now a marginal activity. Less than a century ago, Bohuslän had six thousand fishermen; now it has fewer than one thousand.

The longest and richest herring period occurred in 1749–1808. Once again, it was preceded by a dearth of herring. Pehr Kalm, an explorer, botanist and prominent student of Linnaeus, visited Bohuslän in 1742 and was followed by Linnaeus himself four years later. Both men recorded the existence of mackerel, flounder, skate, prawns, lobster, gurnard, whiting and a myriad other fish species, yet made no mention of herring in their notes at all. But just three years after Linnaeus's visit, the sea was boiling with herring. The electrifying effect on the coastal communities was described by the clergyman and historian Axel Emanuel Holmberg in 1845:

"When the herring appear, the men throw down their ploughs and hoes and hurry to partake in the promised feast, leaving their womenfolk to work in the fields, an occupation the men then deride as a useless

sideline… However, the greatest curse that the belauded herring fishing brings to the province is the extreme immorality that then circulates and which is handed down through subsequent generations. The licentiousness seen in the archipelago during the great fish period in 1747 to 1808 defies description. Violent acts, fornication, cursing and the worst forms of drunkenness were practised day and night. From morning to night the fisherman and worker would stagger round his house, along the jetty and in his boat, and at night the most disgusting orgies took place… When, eventually, the fish were finished, the worst of the riff-raff stayed on and upheld the moral desert which still remains in some areas of the archipelago. Herring fishing has caused similar abominations down the ages. One should therefore not be surprised to hear every upstanding Bohusläner say: 'Please God, let the herring never come.'"

Not all clergymen viewed herring as an iniquitous influence, though. A Bohuslän chaplain, Olof Lundbeck, wrote in 1832:

"He who saw the Bohuslän archipelago twenty-five years ago and would now return to see it again would hardly be able to restrain his tears. It was at its finest then, with costly walls and pilings rising from the sea itself, on which were built the largest salting houses and oil plants. Further along the beach one saw filled storehouses and busy workshops, topped by elegant buildings and thousands of fishing cottages and workers' dwellings. The beaches were alive with people and the sea abounded with flapping sails… All was movement and life, and weighty profits were counted."

Herring fishing was an autumn and early winter activity, during which time labour was in great demand. Every season, some fifteen thousand crofters, farmhands, maids and soldiers would arrive on the West Coast to work as gillers, salters or oil extractors. They may not have earned "weighty profits" but they nevertheless made a tidy wage. In old currency, a salter could earn twenty riksdaler per season, while a maid or farmhand could earn six riksdaler per year.

Herring offal was cooked to make oil used as fuel for street lamps. By the end of the eighteenth century there were 429 oil extraction plants along the coast and the oil was exported as far afield as Paris, where it illuminated the streets during the Revolution.

As the herring fishing reached industrial proportions, environmental concerns started to surface. In 1783, Anders Dahl, a student of Linnaeus, was commissioned by industrialist Clas Alströmer to investigate whether the waste produced by the herring oil plants might be harmful to fish and West Coast harbours.

In what must have been one of history's first environmental impact assessments, Dahl kept a detailed log of what he found. On 18 December 1783 he recorded the sensational observation of a bird, *Alca impennis,*

The *Asta*, sailing from Hållö, is a classic fishing boat, built in 1918 and worked until 1980. Now she carries tourists out to the islands beyond Smögen.

Lobster traps dry in Fjällbacka harbour.

from the quayside of Mollösund, a small fishing hamlet. Apparently attracted by the stench of rotting fish the bird, known as a great auk and never before observed in Sweden, was seen by Dahl feeding on herring offal. The species, which was flightless, was hunted mercilessly for its feathers and became extinct sixty years later. The last living specimen was hacked to death on the island of Eldey, off Iceland, in 1844. Dahl's observation remains the only verified record for Sweden.

When the herring shoals suddenly vanished in about 1808, the party ended, but the West Coast did not this time succumb to its usual bout of post-herring apathy. A whole new range of opportunities were emerging as the Industrial Revolution dawned, and West Coast communities were eager for a slice of the cake.

One new industry was granite quarrying, which started in the 1830s. Bohuslän granite was of first-class quality and the industry benefited too from its ideal location right by the sea. The stone soon became known internationally and was exported all over the world.

At their height, the granite quarries provided livelihoods for ten thousand stonecutters. It was hard and dangerous work, and industrial disputes were frequent. The West Coast stonecutters were early recruits to the fledgling trade union movement, forming their first trade union in 1896. They were also keen participants in temperance societies, with a stonecutters' poll in the early 1900s revealing that one in five was an active member of the temperance movement.

Granite was in due course eclipsed as a building material by asphalt and concrete. Only a few, small granite companies remain in existence today, though the memories of the granite age are preserved for posterity in granite stonework and structures around the country. The herring industry was equally ephemeral, and only one herring oil plant remains intact to this day – at Kålhuvudet, just south of Kyrkesund on the island of Tjörn.

Nowadays, the West Coast, in common with all Sweden's archipelagos and coastal zones, is an area for recreation. Tourism is the big new industry. Fewer and fewer people live all year round on the islands, and during winter the densely packed wooden houses and fishing huts stand mostly empty and idle. But in summer the population skyrockets, and the inhospitable bare slabs of granite transform into inviting spots for swimmers and sunbathers. Yachts and motor boats jostle for space in the harbours.

These are new times. The big draw now is not herring and mackerel but adventure and experience. The archipelago, with its pleasure boats and heaving jetties, has become a theme park. The old fishing hamlets have developed into exclusive summer villages, the old buildings sporting price tags that few fishermen could ever afford.

Red Bohus granite. From Gullmaren north, the bedrock is granite and approximately 800 million years old. South of Gullmaren gneiss, a metamorphic rock about twice as old, predominates.

Three steel-clad lighthouses were built on the West Coast in the 1860s. The first was constructed on Måseskär, south Bohuslän, in 1862.

Harbours and quaysides are no longer polluted by herring offal but by agricultural run-off and untreated sewage, and by emissions from diesel engines, refineries, paper mills, cars, aeroplanes (the list goes on). All this industrial waste is stressing our coastal waters, sometimes to breaking point.

On 9 May 1988, a toxic alga, *Chrysochromulina polyepis*, was discovered in Gullmarsfjorden, a fjord on the Bohuslän coast. In the space of just a few weeks it had contaminated the sea to a depth of ten to fifteen metres along Sweden's entire North Sea coast – from Kullen in Skåne, to the north of Bohuslän and farther on to Stavanger in Norway. Crabs, mussels, fish, ragworm, starfish and other marine organisms died en masse, forming a stinking, rotting mass on the seabed.

On the rocks and skerries, another environmental trauma was played out as harbour seals coughed themselves to death. Fifteen thousand died along the West Coast in the worst epidemic ever to hit the region's seal population.

The two events were unconnected, occurring simultaneously by chance. But they reinforced the impression of a marine environment in distress. The concerns were felt politically, too, and led to the Green Party winning its first-ever seats in parliament at the 1988 general election.

The causes of the toxic algal bloom have never been established, but the mass death of seals was indirectly due to overfishing in the northern Arctic Ocean. During the 1970s and 1980s, millions of tonnes of capelin – a small fish of the smelt family that is a staple for seals, whales and cod – were fished from in the Barents Sea. The quantities were so vast that by 1987 scientists estimated the surviving stock at only a few thousand tonnes.

The capelin were mostly ground into fish fodder and sold to salmon farms, their disappearance from the ocean causing starvation among Greenland seals. Hungry and wasted, the seals undertook a desperate search for food and many reached Norway. In spring 1987 an estimated four hundred thousand Greenland seals were off the Norwegian coast, with some venturing as far south as Swedish waters.

They carried a distemper virus that they were immune to themselves but which was fatal for the local harbour seals they encountered. In the space of a few summer months, eighteen thousand of Europe's thirty thousand harbour seals were wiped out.

Happily, the species rebounded quickly, and when I visited a West Coast colony in September 2001 I counted more than seventy individual seals in an hour. All seemed healthy and none were coughing. It is worth stressing that the distemper virus has not been eradicated, and a new outbreak in 2002 killed twenty two thousand harbour seals. But the fact that the cause was known and people realised it would not wipe out the

Racing Optimist dinghies on the fjord near Tjörn. The third Saturday in August marks the Tjörn Runt yacht race. The tiny Optimists compete the day before.

Vinga. The peaked structure next to the lighthouse is a beacon, erected on this island during the reign of King Karl IX in the early seventeenth century. The first lighthouse was built in 1841; the current tower dates from 1890.

species altogether brought a muted public response and political reaction. Sure enough, in very same month I visited the West Coast seals, the Green Party lost all its parliamentary seats in the general election.

During the 1980s, when ecological disasters seemed to be almost an everyday event, the North Sea was labelled a sea in crisis. A couple of decades on, the tone is less apocalyptic and the prophecies not quite so gloomy. But the environmental emergencies have made us realise that the sea is vulnerable and needs peace and protection.

Gullmarsfjorden, Sweden's largest fjord, was designated as a nature reserve in 1983 and one or two other important coastal areas have followed. Work is currently under way to designate the marine environment of Kosterhavet, between the towns of Strömstad and Grebbestad, as a national park.

It is an area of four hundred and fifty square kilometres, much of it open sea. It would be the first marine national park in Sweden and would be linked to an area of similar size across the border in Norway. If the initiatives go according to plan, the two areas will be officially unveiled as new national parks in September 2009.

A small fishing boat at twilight near Koster. This area is proposed for inclusion in Sweden's first completely marine national park.

Two identical lighthouses were built on Nordkoster in 1850. These were found to be badly placed, and two replacements were built in 1891 on nearby Ursholmen. A group of enthusiasts have renovated the buildings, and the north tower is now working again.

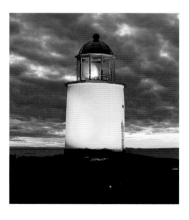

Ursholmen, south of Koster. The twin lighthouses were built in 1891. The northern tower went dark in 1931 after a fire, but the south tower was in use until 2000.

Väderöbod, on Södra Väder-öarna, is Bohuslän's most isolated and perhaps most dramatic lighthouse. Currents are strong here and any number of ship-wrecks is noted in local history. The first lighthouse, built in 1867, was replaced a hundred years later by this red tower.

Hästvam was once a pilot's residence at the far edge of the Fjällbacka archipelago (overleaf).

Menacing eyes in the rock at Ramsvikslandet on the tip of Sotenäset, a popular hiking area within an 800-hectare nature preserve (previous pages).

Old fishing shacks nestle in the bays of Smögen. Almost all have been remodelled into summer cottages. The kilometre-long pier at Smögen is one of the biggest tourist attractions in Sweden, and fresh seafood is still available in the harbour.

Svangens fyr near Resö in northern Bohuslän. The light-house was lit in 1889.

Tugboats *Bonden* and *Boss* help
a supertanker moor at a refinery
in Brofjorden. The harbour at
Lysekil, Sweden's second largest, handles at least five boats a
day of up to 500,000 tonnes.
The refinery meets more than 75
per cent of Sweden's fuel needs
(previous pages).

Gullholmen, outside Orust,
may be Sweden's most densely
built island – some houses
aren't even on the island but
on poles over the water. Gullholmen grew with herring fishing in the eighteenth century,
and still more in the nineteenth
century exporting salted fish to
the United States.

Mollön, outside Orust. Once almost a caricature of west coast life, it's rare these days to see cows grazing on heather (previous pages).

Yacht racing under the new bridge, Tjörnbron. The competing boats meet a tanker of the same type as the *Star Clipper,* which sailed into the bridge on January 19, 1980, toppling a pillar and bringing the entire span down into the water. The new bridge opened in November 1981.

View from Kyrkesund on Tjörn toward Härön. In the nineteenth century, this was one of the most important harbours on the west coast for exporting grain to England. The red warehouse was built in 1847 to store oats, and it was said at the time that London's horse-drawn railways were powered by Swedish feed. Now the warehouse is a restaurant (overleaf).

A sailboat passes the Väcker lighthouse outside Tjurpannan, north of Grebbestad. These waters are feared as the most dangerous on the Bohus coast.

Trying to salvage a dinghy that has broken loose and washed up on the rocks.

The passenger ferry *Hakefjord*
on her way from Rönnäng to
Åstol, the densely built island
south of Tjörn. The first part of
the trip goes through the narrow
Kalvesund channel.

Gothenburg in evening light.
For decades after World War II,
this was one of the world's
leading shipbuilding cities,
home to several large shipyards.
But everything collapsed in the
worldwide shipbuilding crisis of
the 1970s. Now the Gothenburg
Opera, which opened in 1994,
occupies the best spot on the
Göta Älvskajen pier (overleaf).

Asperö in the southern Gothenburg archipelago, viewed from
Rivö to the south. The population of Asperö has quadrupled
since the 1960s to about 440,
with most residents commuting
to the city on the ferry seen to
the right (pp. 54–55).

Varberg Fort and the palatial bathhouse. Construction of the fort began in the thirteenth century. A bathhouse has stood here since 1866, but has fallen victim to the stormy seas more than once. This building from the 1990s is a reproduction of the original.

The twin lighthouses on Nidingen were built in 1832, but as early as 1624 there were simpler towers on this flat, treacherous island. Despite the precautions, ships continued to run aground here into the twentieth century (overleaf).

SOUTH COAST

The only coastline in Sweden to lack an archipelago, the South Coast between Varberg and Åhus is known for its beaches, dunes and sandbanks. People come from all over the country to sunbathe and swim here, and many of the old fishing villages are now popular holiday resorts.

From Varberg, south of Gothenburg, to Åhus in the southern province of Skåne the coastline is flat and fickle. A single word describes it: sand.

At the Getterön nature reserve on the outskirts of Varberg, south of Gothenburg, the islands and rugged granite outcrops of the West Coast give way to the open, sandy vistas of the South Coast. This wind-blown landscape of dunes, sandbanks and beaches is a place for holiday-makers, windsurfers and sun lovers.

From Varberg the coast heads south, swinging east and then north before arriving at Åhus. The only stretch of shoreline in Sweden to lack an archipelago, its flatness puts it at the permanent mercy of the wind and waves. On his visit to Skåne in 1749, the celebrated Swedish naturalist Carl Linneaus reported on the invidious sand that swept in over the fields and meadows:

"Wind-blown sand lay a-plenty on both sides of the river at Åhus… The weather often drives the sand one and a half miles inland, and this can best be observed on the snow in winter-time. Thus the sand makes the rivers shallower and fills the fields and land… Wherever a juniper or willow bush grew on the slopes it was covered in sand like a large tussock, so only the outermost branches were visible."

Drifting sand is a long-standing problem along the South Coast, caused by a low-lying coastal plain and a lack of trees and high vegetation. Of Kämpinge village in south-west Skåne, Linnaeus wrote that it was "greatly plagued by wind-blown sand that whipped into the village like large drifts of snow and ruined the farmland." There seems little doubt that the region has been one of the country's most exposed and windswept parts ever since humans first settled there.

The coastal meadows in this corner of Sweden emerged from the sea during the Bronze Age. Archaeological finds reveal that they were intensively cultivated during that period, suggesting they have probably always been treeless. Even if they were partly wooded for a time, they would not have survived the wholesale felling of forest during the great herring-fishing era in medieval times. Then, up to 100,000 people inhabited the thirty kilometres of coast between Falsterbo and Malmö.

Coastal meadows near Vitemölla, a fishing village north of Kivik. The name refers to the water-powered mill that was once used to grind locally grown grain (p. 60).

Morups Tånge, north of Falkenberg in Halland, is known for its rich variety of birds (pp. 62–63).

Hovs Hallar, one of the few places on the South Coast where the bedrock of the Scandinavian peninsula is exposed. The name Hov comes from a local village, and probably means "temple" or "house of the gods". Hallar is simply a word for "flat rocks" in the local dialect (previous pages).

A boardwalk crosses the beach at Sandhammaren in south-eastern Skåne. This is one of the few areas in southern Sweden where the sand dunes remain undeveloped. The sensitive, nearly barren dune, some five kilometres long, is a nature reserve. Once upon a time, though, these sand reefs were a nearly invisible nightmare for seafarers, and pirates would lie in wait here to plunder any ships that ran aground.

The lie of the land changed little until the mid-eighteenth century, when widespread planting of pines took place in an effort to shield the coastline from the elements. The main aim of the plantations was to prevent wind-borne sand from spoiling prime arable land. Native Scots pine did not grow well on the outer dunes so dwarf mountain-pine was planted instead, creating "impenetrable thickets the height of a man," in the words of one writer.

These days, the beaches and coastal meadows of southern Skåne are no longer rising from the sea. Instead, the sea chips away at the coastline, shifting dunes and sandbanks east or north along the coast depending on how the currents run. No other part of Sweden loses so much land to erosion as Skåne and the southernmost part of Halland province.

The peninsula of Skanör and Falsterbo, which forms the south-westernmost tip of the country, is home to a peculiarly shaped sandbank known as Måkläppen. Though it dates back to the Bronze Age, Måkläppen is constantly evolving and changing in shape. At one time a round island of sand, it became a narrow reef of sand before morphing into its current shape – a hairpin-shaped spit now joined to the land.

Back in the Middle Ages people lived on Måkläppen, building huts on the sand from where they fished the bountiful herring stocks. Marked as an island on seventeenth century nautical charts, Måkläppen has always posed a threat to passing mariners. The name comes from *måge* (the Danish word for gull) and *kläpp* (reef), and to this day Måkläppen is a haven for gulls and other birds. Eider, shelduck, mute swan, oystercatcher, avocet and sandwich tern are among twenty nine species that breed there.

Måkläppen is also an important breeding ground for seals, and together with the island of Hallands Väderö is home to the only seal colony on the South Coast. Uniquely, both grey seals and harbour seals rear their young here. In 1899, a doctor and ornithologist named Paul Rosenius founded the Association for the Protection of Måkläppen's Birdlife, the country's very first nature conservation organisation. Its first move was to take out a lease on Måkläppen from the municipal authority in Skanör and Falsterbo and declare it a protected area. In 1971, Måkläppen was officially designated a nature reserve and is now closed to the public from 1 March to 31 October.

Måkläppen's protected status was put to the test in the late 1980s, when Saab announced plans to build a new factory in Malmö harbour. The car manufacturer's plan was to fill in part of the harbour area to create parking and test tracks using sand extracted from a sandbank five kilometres off the shore of Måkläppen. The idea was to fill the harbour with three million cubic metres of the finest quartz sand, which would have entailed digging a trench six metres deep, fifty metres wide and

Måkläppen is a remarkable sand reef near Falsterbo that constantly changes shape under the influence of the currents and waves. The reef is vital for the local wildlife, and is especially favoured by seals.

The Hallands Väderö lighthouse is a thirteen-metre-high, slightly tapered iron pipe. Built in 1884, it was automated in 1964.

one kilometre long. The sandbank's closeness to Måkläppen meant there was a potential risk of damage to the nature reserve, though no formal research was carried out.

Saab wanted to get the factory project off the ground as soon as possible and promptly gained governmental approval. But the plans ran into fierce local opposition in Skanör and Falsterbo, and the municipal authorities succeeded in halting the initiative. Måkläppen was left in peace and the protected zone extended to include the sandbank offshore.

Today, the Skåne County Administrative Board showcases the coastal waters off Falsterbo as "an area of shifting sands with few equivalents in Sweden" and identifies the sandbank once targeted by Saab as the country's premier breeding ground for turbot. For its part, Saab went on to build its plant in Malmö (without the coastal sand), but just 200 cars rolled off the production line before the plant was closed. It is now the Malmö Exhibition and Convention Centre.

In only a few places does higher land intersperse the flat South Coast: the island of Ven, Glumslövs Backar outside Helsingborg, Kåseberga, and the rocky cliffs of Stenshuvud, Kullaberg and Hallandsåsen.

Beyond the rugged shores of Hallandsåsen (the Halland ridge) lies the island of Hallands Väderö, said to have Sweden's mildest climate. Its woodlands of oak, lime and beech are fringed with dense patches of hawthorn, blackthorn, buckthorn, rose hip and Guelder rose, mixed with brambles and honeysuckle. The island is something of a relic – a living testament to what the Skåne coastline looked like in ancient times.

"Skåne was once covered by forests like these, growing down right to the shoreline," wrote the zoologist and author Carl Fries in 1950. "Nowadays, the beaches are bordered by open land and arable fields. Nothing remains to remind us of how things used to look, save the precious island of Hallands Väderö. Here, woodland still skirts the coastline and the rich, untamed nature beneath the canopy has a primeval feel."

Various people, mostly harbour pilots, stonemasons and lighthouse keepers, have lived on Hallands Väderö throughout its history, but today the island is uninhabited. Since 1958 it has been managed as a nature reserve.

To the south, the Kullaberg peninsula juts out into the Kattegatt, standing sentry over the confluence of the salty North Sea waters with the brackish Baltic. The sea water north of this neck of land contains three and a half per cent salt; south of it this falls to one per cent. The percentage gradually declines as the Baltic swings north, dropping to just 0.2 per cent in the innermost reaches of the Gulf of Bothnia.

The South Coast fishing industry is less prominent than on the West Coast. The fishing hamlets are more modest and have closer ties to agriculture, many once being part of large estates. For instance, the fishing

The furrowed rock of Kullaberg is topped by Kullens fyr, Sweden's highest lighthouse at 78.5 metres above the sea. It is also the most powerful, with a visible range exceeding 27 nautical miles.

villages of Mölle and Arild on Kullaberg were once part of the powerful Krapperup estate and required to supply the nobles with a fixed proportion of their catch and to labour in the fields.

Arild also had links with the Archbishop of Lund, who had fishing rights there along with similar entitlements in Barsebäck and Falsterbo. In medieval times, Arild was known as *Hellij Aruitz leije* (Holy Arild).

The fishing hamlets of Beddinge and Smyge, east of Trelleborg, also belonged to large estates and the now-defunct Knäbäck near Simrishamn on the eastern seaboard became an important fishing centre after coming under the stewardship of the nobleman owner of two nearby estates. Knäbäck's star later waned, and when it was adopted as the headquarters of the Skåne Tank Regiment its fishing roots all but disappeared among the roar of Centurion tanks.

Once a major centre for herring fishing, the South Coast is nowadays perhaps better known for its eel. Whether boiled, fried, smoked, grilled or prepared in the time-honoured way on a bed of straw, eel has a special place in the region's cuisine. The species itself is enigmatic and mysterious. It passes the South Coast in late summer and autumn on its way out from the Baltic Sea to return to the Sargasso Sea, and it is then that fishermen set their traps. But eels will not enter the pots in moonlight, so the fishermen must venture out in when there is a new moon and it is pitch black, conditions known locally as "eel darkness". Though the season starts in August, the prime eel fishing season is during the long nights of October and November.

Grilled eel is a speciality in Skåne and cooked over an open fire. Smoked eel is also popular and considered a must on every Christmas dinner table. Certainly, eel is the economic mainstay for small-scale South Coast fishermen. Rather more surprisingly, eel is the third most valuable species for the entire Swedish fishing industry, after cod and herring.

But eel fishing is in crisis. In the 1950s, experts started noting a decline in the number of young eels, or elvers, reaching the West Coast and in the 1980s the decrease accelerated, not just in Sweden but across Central and Southern Europe. By the late 1990s numbers had dropped so low that the species was classified as acutely threatened.

The causes of the decline are unclear, though suspicion focuses on overfishing and disruption to spawning grounds in the Sargasso Sea. Proposals are now afoot to limit the fishing season and for eel-fishing nations to work together to increase the numbers of adult, or silver, eels that leave northern Europe on their return migration to the Sargasso Sea. The aim is for forty per cent of the eels that would migrate successfully, were it not for human interference to actually do so.

These days, cod and herring fishing is only a marginal livelihood on the

Eel has long been central to food culture in Skåne, but overfishing is a problem and catches are under strict quotas.

Poles used to hang nets and other eel fishing gear at Friseboda in the Hanöbukten bay.

South Coast. Classic fishing communities like Träslövsläge, Haverdal, Tylösand, Torekov, Arild, Mölle, Ålabodarna, Barsebäck, Skanör, Falsterbo, Abbekås, Skillinge and Kivik are no longer famed for their harbours and fishing shacks but for their exclusive waterfront real estate. An advert headlined "Live in Skåne" in the Svenska Dagbladet newspaper on 2 May 2007 read:

"Weekend house in quiet and congenial location close to Arild, S:t Arild Golf Club and the countryside and sea. Delightful garden of 1,145 square metres with small guest-house. Two bedrooms, living room and kitchen in living area of 46 square metres. Built in 1960. Price 1,775,000 kronor or highest offer."

Where once sand plagued the coastline, it now attracts people to it; and where livelihoods once depended on cod and herring, they now rely on pristine beaches, rolling sand dunes and crisp sea air instead.

Beach huts among the sand dunes at Falsterbo Strand – mementos of the intensive beach scene of the early 1900s.

Bjärehalvön overlooks Torekov, Hallands Väderö and Kattegatt. This peninsula enjoys a mild climate and is famous for its new potatoes, gardens and golf courses (overleaf).

The golf course at Barsebäck, with lush greens and vegetation-choked water. In the distance hazardsis a glimpse of Danish Sjælland.

The western shore of the island of Ven faces southern Öresund. "Ven" is old Danish and means something like "floating in foam". But the island has been Swedish since 1660 and now belongs to the municipality of Landskrona. The island's soil is extremely rich, and the population of about 370 souls subsist on agriculture, ice cream, tourism and, perhaps soon, whiskey. A local distillery is under construction.

When it was built in 1909, the Grand Hôtel in Mölle, at Kullaberg, was breathlessly described as a den of iniquity because men and women bathed together, still scandalous behaviour for many. German Kaiser Wilhelm II vacationed in Mölle in 1907, giving a big lift to the local tourist industry right up until the outbreak of World War I. A century later, tourism is back (previous pages).

The mighty pylons of the Öresund Bridge between Sweden and Denmark, 204 metres high and with a clearance of 57 metres. The bridge opened in 2000 and is considered a powerful economic engine for the entire Öresund region.

An easterly gale hits Hanöbukten, rolling waves up a beach in the Stenshuvud National Park, south of Kivik.

The lighthouse at Falsterbo was built in 1793, but the site has been used as a warning post for far longer than that: Fires were built here as early as the fourteenth century to warn sailors. Of course, this was all part of Denmark in those days.

Turning Torso, the twisted skyscraper in Malmö that has become a proud postmodern landmark for sailors approaching the city.

Falsterbokanalen, a practical
shortcut through treacherous
shoals, was completed in the
summer of 1941.

Morning swim in the Kattegatt
from a dock at Torekov on the
tip of the Bjäre peninsula.

The beaches at Falsterbo
sometimes suffer the effects of
agricultural over-fertilisation:
rotting piles of green algae
(overleaf).

Skanör harbour. This popular
guest harbour was first constructed
in the late nineteenth century.

From the air, this swimming pier at Riberborgsbadet looks like it is out to sea. But this is in fact central Malmö, between Turning Torso and the Öresund Bridge.

Cows graze in the morning mist at Kåseberga on the south coast of Skåne (previous pages).

The fishing village of Brantevik, south of Simrishamn. A few pleasure boats and a fishing boat are in the little harbour today, but this was once the busiest port in Sweden. In the early twentieth century, the village owned 118 ships, far more than Stockholm or Gothenburg. The outbreak of war in 1914 changed Brantevik forever.

Boat launch at Stenshuvud, south of Kivik. The steepest cliffs in Sweden are found near here, rising 97 metres above sea level. Stenshuvud is also the name of the national park established here in 1986 (overleaf).

Friseboda nature reserve in Hanöbukten (pp. 98–99)

EAST COAST

The southern and central Baltic is an area of shifting beauty and character. Narrow in some places and deep in others, the coastline is a world of rocky headlands and green forests. Stretching from Åhus to Trosa, it is dotted by fishing hamlets and small farms. Sparsely populated, it comes alive in the summer months.

The Listerlandet peninsula in Blekinge province marks the end of the sandy South Coast and the start of the East Coast archipelago, a scattered collection of islands, islets and skerries stretching all the way to the Gulf of Bothnia in the uppermost Baltic.

Sparsely spread and narrow in some places, and densely packed and wide in others, the islands are an exceptional marine environment. Offshore islands are found in many places around the world. But the Swedish archipelago, with its smooth slabs of gneiss and granite, millions of years old, shaped by the retreating glaciers and the incessant pounding of the sea and rising clear above the water, is unique in geological terms. Usually, such ancient bedrock is covered by younger sedimentary rock. And though old by geological standards, the landscape is still evolving due to the ongoing process of land uplift. Thus sunken reefs emerge gradually from the sea, becoming skerries, then islets and finally islands. And existing islands grow steadily taller as they are lifted above the water. The rate of annual uplift increases as you go north, starting at a couple of millimetres per year in Blekinge, reaching five millimetres in Stockholm and peaking at one centimetre on the High Coast of Ångermanland.

In this book, the East Coast covers the stretch of archipelago between Karlshamn in Blekinge and Bråviken Bay outside Norrköping. It spans three different geological zones: the Blekinge coast with its low, moraine-rich, leafy islands; the flatlands of the Kalmar Sound, which share a common ancestry with the soft, sedimentary rock of Öland; and the fjord-like archipelagos of northern Småland and Östergötland.

Compared to the West Coast, the East Coast has a richer flora and is less built-up. It lacks the bare cliffs and crags and densely clustered fishing villages of the West Coast. Its fishing grounds are less plentiful, too.

But it has other assets. Unlike the West Coast, where many islands have lost their woodlands to firewood and timber, the East Coast islands have retained their leafy forests. Blekinge archipelago is known for its deciduous woods, and the larger islands in particular retain generous canopies. "The oak here on the Blekinge coast has a strength, weight and all-embracing crown like nowhere else in Sweden," wrote the noted

Ice-smoothed flat rocks with granite boulders covered with wave-tossed bladder wrack – a typical scene on the Swedish East Coast. Misterhult archipelago in northern Småland (p. 100).

Almö in Listerby archipelago in Blekinge. A giant oak stretches its protective branches over the boulders in the field. Almö is known for its grazed pastures featuring juniper bushes and oak trees, and is part of a larger nature reserve that encompasses almost the entire Listerby inner archipelago. (pp. 102–103).

Harstena in Gryt archipelago is perhaps the best-known island on the Swedish East Coast. The first known inhabitant paid rent to the Swedish Crown in the form of eight pounds of seal blubber, 40 perch and ten eggs. Today, people make their living from letting cottages, nature conservation and operating boat taxis. At the end of the nineteenth century more than 80 people lived on the island. Today, there are four left and the future is uncertain (previous pages).

Nightfall at Trässö in Tjust archipelago. Trässö is a typical rocky coastal islet with sparse vegetation and no buildings, and is essentially untouched.

twentieth century zoologist Carl Fries. "The venerable oaks shading the manor house at Skärva are the most beautiful you can see."

The oak trees provide a home for the magnificent stag beetle, the largest of its kind in Europe and a species that requires dead, rotting oak wood – something that Blekinge's woods provide more of than anywhere else in the country. That so many oaks were left to grow to maturity is remarkable considering that Blekinge and its coastline has long been the centre of the Swedish navy and attendant industries. In its heyday in the eighteenth century, the naval port of Karlskrona was the largest city in the country, built as a redoubt from which to repel Danish attacks. Insatiable demand for shipbuilding timber during that era saw many oaks fall to the axe, but enough survived for the coast to retain its character.

Utklippan lighthouse marks the East Coast's southernmost point. The lighthouse itself has been fully automatic since the last keeper departed in 1972. Thanks to its sheltered harbour and isolated location in Hanö Bay, Utklippan island is a favourite stopover both for sailors and migratory birds. It also marks the start of the King Valdemar sailing channel, the oldest such route in the country. The distance to Kalmar was in the Middle Ages expressed as ten "seamiles" (equivalent to four nautical miles, or the distance that a crew could row without a break).

That we are able to retrace the route of the channel is due to entries in King Valdemar's land register, kept in the mid-thirteenth century by Bishop Thorkil of Reval, present-day Tallinn. King Valdemar founded Reval in 1222 after leading a series of successful crusades to Estonia. The king and his army sailed to Estonia via the Utklippan-Kalmar channel, passing the archipelagos of northern Småland, Östergötland, Södermanland and Stockholm before crossing the Baltic to Estonia via the Åland islands.

In reality, the sailing channel almost certainly predates King Valdemar's time. After Utklippan and nearby Utlängan, Bishop Thorkil named Bergkvara, a town south of Kalmar which is one of the oldest harbours and mercantile centres on the East Coast (and for that matter anywhere along the Swedish coast). It is known to date back to the Viking era, suggesting that the same channel used by King Valdemar was used by the Vikings before him.

Just up the coast is Påbonäs, a medieval fort built as an outpost to guard against Danish marauders. It is here that the Atlantic herring (*sill* in Swedish) which occurs on the West and South coasts gives way to the Baltic herring, a smaller subspecies (*strömming*).

The seafarer then passes the historic city of Kalmar, where the union between the three kingdoms of Sweden, Denmark and Norway under a single monarch was signed in 1397.

The union lasted for one hundred and twenty-six years until it was dis-

Fish farming in Ronneby archipelago. Go Fish in Sweden AB has been farming rainbow trout here since 1984, totalling 240 tonnes a year, which is a lot for Sweden whose annual production totals seven thousand tonnes, which can be compared with Norway with 460,000 tonnes of salmon – the country's second biggest export commodity after oil.

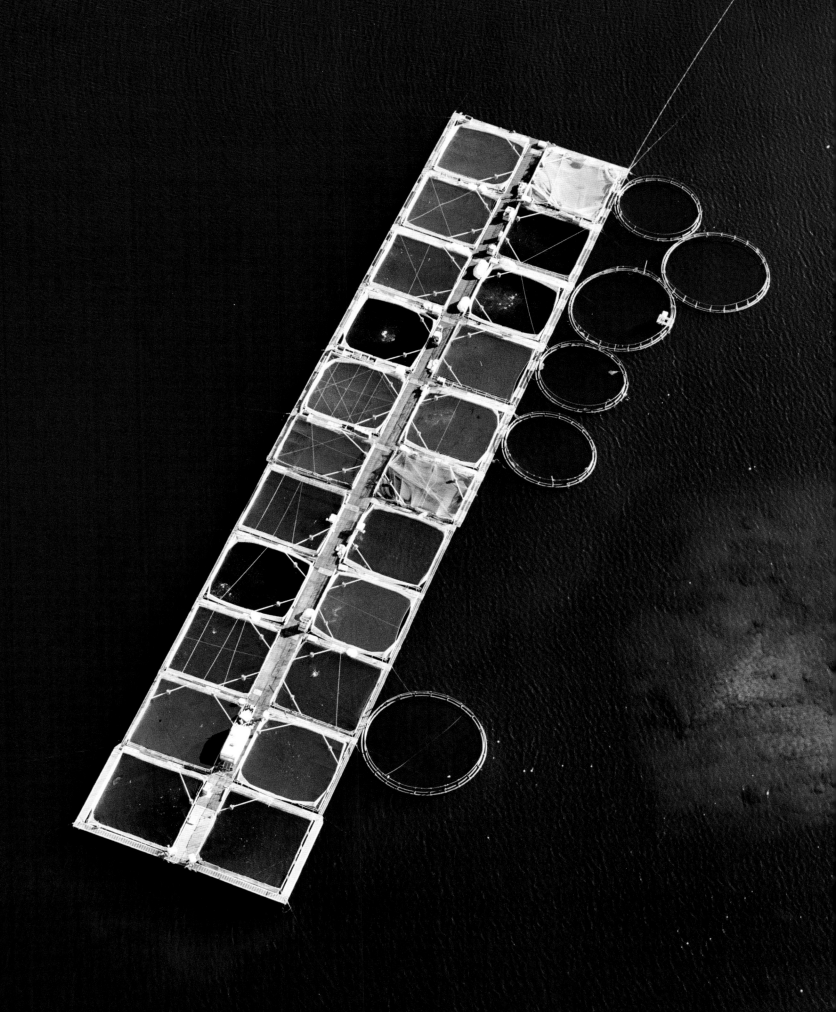

solved in 1524, the year after Gustav Vasa was crowned Swedish king.

Heading north, the next stop is Runnö, a small island in the Kalmar Sound thought to have been inhabited and farmed for at least a thousand years. Remains of medieval homesteads can still be seen today, and it seems likely that King Valdemar and his navy would have called in here on their voyages to and from Estonia.

Invaders from Denmark and other countries plundered Runnö in the seventeenth century, razing its farms and settlements. But the homes and buildings were rebuilt, and two hundred years later the island had a population of almost one hundred, mostly fishermen, farmers and pilots. The island has ten farmsteads and, unlike in many other areas of Sweden, these were not parcelled up, but run semi-communally from two villages, Sörgården and Norrgården. People lived here until well into the 1950s, but today the island has no full-time residents. Though up to a hundred people spend their summers here, Runnö's fate mirrors that of so many small islands along the East Coast. In the space of just four or five decades, all the island's inhabitants either left or died, and the traditional way of life based on farming and fishing disappeared with them. In their wake, property prices have soared as the island has become a popular summer holiday resort.

The next stop in King Valdemar's footsteps is Spårö outside Västervik, a towering island with dramatic granite cliffs and an eighteenth century whitewashed lighthouse. In his 1644 handbook for sailors in the Baltic Sea, Johan Månsson, the senior navigation officer of the Swedish Admiralty, gave the following advice on how to negotiate the waters round Spårö:

"When the wind cometh from the North and thou wisheth to enter Idhesund, thou must sail so that thou dost have the peak of Sporberg, whereon the beacon stands, to thy west south west."

Spårö lies roughly halfway between Misterhult and Tjust, the two main archipelagos on the Småland coast and an island kingdom of no fewer than ten thousand islands, islets and skerries. The coastline here is jagged and known for its long, fjord-like inlets and bays.

The Misterhult archipelago begins where the narrow string of moraine islands in the Kalmar Sound gives way once more to granite outcrops. A jumbled and complex network of islands and low-lying rocks, its waters can be treacherous for the unwary sailor. Many a brig, schooner and steamer lie wrecked beneath the sea. Much of the archipelago was declared a nature reserve in the 1960s, and today it is a paradise for canoeists. There is certainly no better way to explore this most peaceful and unspoilt of all Sweden's archipelagos.

Historically, the area was only sparsely populated and most of the islands are uninhabited. The busiest was Örö, which had a community of

Wild orchids, saxifrage and wild pansies – all typical wild flowers from the archipelago. The photo is from Lammskär in the Sankt Anna archipelago, but similar shoreline pastures can be found everywhere. The lime-rich soils give the East Coast islands a wide range of flora, with orchids in the starring role.

Utklippan is strategically situated near the naval base at Karlskrona. It was built in 1840 on top of a fort designed to protect the coast against enemy attacks.

sixty fishermen, seal hunters, wildfowlers and farmers at its peak in the mid-nineteenth century. Only two people now remain there permanently, eking out a living from eel fishing and tourism.

Beyond Misterhult lie the fertile islands of the Tjust archipelago. And past them you find the rougher, barer islands of Gryt and then the archipelagos of Sankt Anna and Arkö. A little further north is Bråviken Bay and the end of the East Coast. For reasons that are not entirely clear, the stretch from Tjust to Bråviken is known as the Blue Coast. Perhaps someone thought the name would appeal to tourists. But they need not have bothered; the magic and allure of the archipelago is already there in the old place names.

Tjust, pronounced "Schoost", comes from the Old Norse word for violence and was probably taken from the gushing river at Tingstad, a small village between the towns of Västervik and Valdemarsvik. Tingstad is now four kilometres or so from the coast, but geologists say it would have stood at the water's edge in around the year 200 AD. After that, it slowly became detached from the sea by land uplift.

Though Tjust can trace its name back some two thousand years, it would be unrecognisable to people of that era. Back then, the sea level was eight metres higher than today and many of the islands and skerries on current maps lay submerged beneath the sea, only becoming visible when the sea level dropped.

Gryt is one of the East Coast's best known archipelagos. In Old Norse a *gryt* was a pile of stones or stony ground, and this is an apt description for the bare rocks and outcrops that characterise the Gryt archipelago.

St. Anna, the mother of the Virgin Mary, is the patron saint of seafarers, and in 1383 the inhabitants of the community of north Hammarkind received permission to build a chapel in her honour. The local parish, and later the entire archipelago, took their names from the chapel. The islands of Sankt Anna are quite different in character from those to the south. The inner islands of Yxnö, Torön, Gränsö, Norra Finnö and Södra Finnö are large and fertile, and here farming rather than fishing was the traditional mainstay. Connected to the mainland by bridge, they teem with tourists during the summer months and have seen property prices shoot skywards as a result. Beyond them lies a labyrinthine, ten-kilometre-wide band of islets, skerries and rocks that can pose a serious navigational challenge to the inexperienced sailor.

After King Valdemar's crusaders passed Spårö they reached Torrö in the north of the Tjust archipelago, five "seamiles" away. Records show that a sixteen-metre-high cross stood here in the twelfth century, erected perhaps to commemorate the Estonian crusades. Though the cross later disappeared, a replica was put in place on the same spot and consecrated by Bishop Martin Lönnebo in 1994 in a ceremony marking the

Morning calm in Bergkvara harbour in southern Kalmarsund. The grain silo was built by the farmers' union in Södra Möre in the 1950s, but it soon became outdated and is now empty apart from a small store of fuel pellets. The other buildings sometimes house a harbour office and wind-power exhibition. Bergkvara is one of the oldest harbours along the East Coast, and may date from the Viking Age. At the end of the nineteenth century, the shipping and navigation industries were of major importance. The harbour today (2007) is experiencing a strong renaissance due to all the timber being shipped out after being felled by two recent hurricanes in Sweden.

A sailboat passes the Skomakarn light on Marsholmen in Tjust archipelago.

official launch of the King Valdemar Sailing Channel project, an initiative to recreate the route taken by the crusaders and make the area a tourist and cultural attraction.

After Torrö, the crusaders would have reached Kvädö, located at the head of a narrow and fjord-like inlet which later gained the appropriate name of Valdemarsviken (vik means "bay"). According to the ancient sagas, the bay was named after a King Valdemar who sought refuge there from enemy forces with his fleet. Whether it refers to King Valdemar the crusader or another, earlier King Valdemar is not known.

Alas, the toponymists who specialise in researching place names have dented this romantic account, claiming instead that the bay takes its name from nearby Vammar farm, which in turn drew its name from Wagmare, meaning shallow bay in Old Norse. How Wagmare made the leap to Valdermarsviken is unclear, but a nautical chart from 1653 identifies the bay as Waldemars Wiken, so maybe there is more than a grain of truth in the royal link after all.

The latter half of the twentieth century brought a radical and dramatic transformation to archipelago life. Communities which for centuries had resided on the islands, making a living from fishing, hunting and farming, all but vanished in the space of a few short decades. In their place came summer tourists. All the populated islands suffered the same fate, and today only a few scattered homes are occupied year-round. Harstena in the Gryt archipelago, perhaps the best known island on the east coast, is an example. It had fifty inhabitants in the 1950s. Today, only a single family remains, subsisting from running taxi boats, doing conservation work and filing weather reports.

The 1950s heralded the start of the industrialisation of the small-scale fishing that used to support numerous local island communities. Nowadays, a handful of large trawler companies dominate the fishing industry, and almost all other fishing (with one or two exceptions) is classed as sea angling. Few people hunt anymore and most agriculture is carried out under conservation projects rather than for food production. Times have certainly changed.

As has the sea. The waters are not as clear as they were fifty years ago and an invasion of blanketweed algae has forced the underwater forests of kelp seaweed into retreat. Fish species like pike, perch and Baltic herring have declined, almost disappearing in some areas, though sprat numbers have risen strongly. Populations of eider, velvet scoter and other ducks have decreased, while cormorants have increased dramatically and are now abundant along the coast.

Regular visitors to the archipelago know what it is like to walk down to the jetty one summer's day to find the sea heaving with a soup-like mass of poisonous blue-green algae. The unnerving sight of these algal

Yellow stonecrop and orange-yellow lichen on a rock in the Sankt Anna archipelago.

Kråkelund beacon in the Misterhult archipelago north of Oskarshamn. This unusual seamark was constructed in 1849 and is still intact, although in need of renovation.

blooms tells us that the marine ecology is under strain and no longer in balance. The precise causes have yet to be fully established, but hot weather, high nutrient levels and overfishing of cod are seen as the most likely culprits.

On the plus side, water clarity has improved slightly in the last few years and kelp has recolonised some of its former haunts. The majestic white-tailed eagle has also staged a comeback after its numbers plummeted in the 1950s and 1960s due to pesticides and heavy metals in its fish prey. Near the island of Kvädö, a programme to save the eagle was launched twenty five years ago and included a ban on all fishing and imposition of an exclusion zone for motor boats. As a result, the surrounding waters have twice as many – and much larger – pike than in surrounding areas. The same goes for perch. It just goes to show that the sea can bounce back if we give it time.

The islands of Tjust, of which Kvädö is one, have been less touched by development than the Gryt and Sankt Anna archipelagos due to the feudal-type structures that held sway there for centuries. Powerful landowners declined to divide up their land, thereby ensuring that the islands avoided the fate of being parcelled up into summer-house plots.

Preserving valuable countryside and nature remains a difficult and delicate task in today's world. But many of the East Coast's islands and inlets now have nature reserve protection, and armed with this they can look forward to retaining their special appeal to canoeists, walkers, sailors, long-distance skaters, skate-sailors and all who love the great outdoors.

The lighthouse on one of the Kuggvik skerries north of Arkö at the mouth of Bråviken has been operating since 1937. This was the first lighthouse in Sweden to be equipped with solar cells: in 1983 the acetylene gas equipment was replaced by four solar panels and a nickel-cadmium battery, giving the lighthouse a reserve running time of three to four months. In other words, the lighthouse could operate all winter without being recharged. The result was such a success that within a short time the Swedish Maritime Administration had equipped 445 lighthouses with solar cells.

Hanö in Hanö Bay. The island, called Högö when it was under Danish rule, has been a seasonal fishing base since prehistoric times, and did not have a settled population until the nineteenth century. The lighthouse was built in 1869, and the lighthouse keepers and fishermen created a lively village of 250 inhabitants. In 1981, the lighthouse was automated and the fishing became industrialised. Today some 30 people live on Hanö (overleaf).

The Utklippan lighthouse in Karlskrona archipelago. This is Sweden's most southerly island group, and its harbour is a longed-for destination of many long-distance sailors. The first light, a simple arrangement with the fire in a metal basket at the end of a long pole, was put in service in 1789, and in 1870 an iron tower like the ones designed by Gustav von Heidenstam was added. The lighthouse staff lived on the island until 1972. There are no trees on Utklippan but the rare natterjack lives on the islands, as does the even rarer green-speckled toad. No one knows how the toads came here. (p. 120–121).

Karlskrona Maritime Museum on the island of Stumholmen (centre). The full-rigged ship *Jarramas* and the minesweeper *Bremön* are berthed at the quay. The *Jarramas* was the last sailing ship to be built at the Karlskrona naval dockyard and was the last full-rigged ship in the Swedish navy, in active service until 1946. The name is Turkish and means "the playful one". That was also the name of a frigate launched by King Karl XII in 1716. The *Bremön* was launched in 1940 and carried out many difficult missions during World War II (previous pages).

In the summer, parts of Kalmarsund Park in Kalmar become a popular swimming spot.

Kalmar Castle, at one time the "key" to the Swedish kingdom and its most southerly outpost in the Baltic Sea, is now a museum. The first defensive tower was built in the twelfth century and was greatly reinforced by King Gustav Vasa. In 1397, Queen Margareta signed the Treaty of the Union of Kalmar here. The union lasted for just over half a century, after which the castle became a cornerstone of Sweden's national defence. After a period of decay it was restored in the 1920s, the drawbridge was replaced and the moat dug out again.

Early morning among the skerries outside Oskarshamn (previous pages).

The Dämman lighthouse in the middle of Kalmarsund, five kilometres off the Mönsterås Bruk pulp mill. The site was originally an underwater rock, which was built up to become an island in 1872. The original lighthouse was decommissioned in 1968 and replaced by a concrete lighthouse fixed to the seabed. The old lighthouse has been renovated and expanded and turned into a hotel and restaurant with a helicopter pad, natural pool, large wine cellar and Italian marble on the floors.

Blå Jungfrun (Blue Virgin) in northern Kalmarsund. Originally it was called Blåkulla (Blue Mountain), but in Swedish folklore that was the place where witches traditionally gathered, so the local people began to call it "the Virgin" instead. Gradually, the two names merged to become the Blue Virgin – although it is not blue at all, but rather red, coloured by a rock called rapakivi granite.

Örö in Misterhult archipelago. This was once a lively eel fishing and piloting community. In the 1860s more than 60 people lived here, but now there are only two permanent residents, making a modest living off tourism. The island is known for its deciduous forest and is sometimes called the island of flowers, the island of nightingales or the pearl of the Småland skerries.

Jungfrusund in thr Tjust archipelago. Between Flatvarp and Väderskär the navigation channel runs along a narrow sound right up to the old fishing huts on Sundsholmen and Jungfruskär, which now has no buildings on it. The only hut on the skerry was moved to Stora Askö in 1942 (overleaf).

Missjö archipelago in Sankt Anna, a far-reaching realm of small islands, islets, rocks and skerries – a nightmare for sailors and a paradise for seabirds and seals. A large area, more than 1,800 hectares stretching from Tyrislöt and out to the farthermost seal rocks, has been a marine nature reserve since 2001. The main beneficiaries are the seabirds, as this is a nesting ground for such species as the skua, velvet skoter, turnstone, black guillemot, mute swan, sheldrake, greater black-backed gull, arctic tern, and red-reasted merganser (pp. 134–135).

ÖLAND AND GOTLAND

These two large Baltic islands are worlds of their own, with a geology and flora entirely different from the mainland. Calcareous soil and an ancient tradition of livestock grazing have sculpted an Arcadian-like landscape of rich floral meadows. The islands' early prosperity was built on livestock farming and trade, but the growing tourism industry is a major earner nowadays.

The two large Baltic islands of Öland and Gotland are unlike anywhere else along Sweden's coast. Their geology is unique and so is their landscape. Flowers and birds thrive in abundance, drawing botanists and ornithologists from across Sweden and beyond.

All Sweden's coastal islands except the moraine islands of the far north are bedrock outcrops – hills and mounds of smooth gneiss and granite formed between one and two million years ago. All, that is, apart from Öland and Gotland, which are made of much younger rock. Unlike bedrock, which has a volcanic origin, Öland and Gotland rest on sedimentary layers of sand, clay, marlstone and limestone, which formed on the sea-bed during the Cambrian, Ordovician och Silurian periods between six hundred and four hundred million years ago.

The sediments were formed in a sea so much warmer than the Baltic of today that it was home to coral-building marine creatures and other tropical species. Geologists believe Öland, Gotland, and indeed the whole of Fennoscandia during the Cambrian era, were much further south than they are today – as far as South Africa , in fact. By the Silurian Age they had moved northwards, but were still only just north of the Equator.

Whether shifts in the Earth's tectonic plates or the angle of its axis – or other factors – caused this migration is a matter of debate. But we know it happened, partly because the islands' sediments contain fossils dating back to those eras. On 27 June 1741, the Swedish botanist Carl Linnaeus was spellbound on finding large numbers of fossilised organisms on the beach at Kappelshamn in northern Gotland: "We collected fossils for hours on the west beach. Sometimes we found large numbers of *conchitae striatae* (grooved mussels) and *cochlitae* (molluscs), some of them very plain, others adorned with a shell and still others filled with crystals."

On the east beach at Kappelhamn Linnaeus discovered a fascinating coral environment:

"I call them the coral beaches, the very wide white and grey pebble beaches to the east of Kappelshamn. We were greatly surprised since each and every stone was nothing less than a coral, known as *Madrepora*.

Early morning in Sundre on southern Gotland (p. 136).

The hamlet of Helgumannen on northern Fårö, was once a centre for cod fishing (previous pages).

Raukar at Byarum during a storm over Öland. A *rauk* is a rock formation carved by the sea.

This famous rock formation at Gamle Hamn on north-west Fårö is called "the Dog" or "the Coffeepot".

Whatever the amount of exquisite coral a man may want for his art and stone collection, he need look no further. There is so much here that anyone in the world could get a cartload. The beach was undulated like a ridged field, with long, low, bumpy ridges parallel to the harbour. They were all made of coral pebbles thrown together, but the further inland they were, the more mixed they were with soil. This place gave us the clearest example of land elevation whereby these corals, or *Madrepores*, which can only grow in the depths of the sea, are thrown onto the beaches, thereby increasing the land mass.

Thus Linnaeus believed the sea threw up coral onto the beach and thereby built up the land. But he did not know the fossiled molluscs' true age and interpreted the process backwards. In actual fact, millions of years of erosion were the key factor underpinning the land's gradual rise.

Öland and Gotland started life on the sea-bed. From the Cambrian to the Silurian periods they were under water, amassing enormous layers of sand, clay and dead animals and plants over the course of millions of years. As time passed, the layers became sediment and hardened into sandstone, limestone and marlstone. In his 1964 book *De stora öarna i Östersjön* (Large Baltic Islands), author Carl Fries described what happened next:

"The Silurian Sea became steadily shallower and the Swedish land emerged above sea level. The erosive forces began to do their work. Rock was pounded into pieces and taken back into the bosom of the sea. Prior to the modern era the land was carried away as the heavy glaciers scoured the rocky surface, carrying huge amounts of stone and gravel in their wake. Thus the sea deposits were destroyed and swept away by the forces of time…"

These are the forces that fashioned Öland's and Gotland's preciptous cliffs, limestone formations and pebble beaches, though what we see today are just the weathered and worn remains of vast sea-bed sediments accumulated during hundreds of millions of years.

The islands' flora differs greatly from the archipelagos. The calcareous soil supports a diversity and richness that only Skåne can match. Flowers grow in unmatched profusion in the dry, sunny and mild climate. Two species of sun-loving rock-rose, *Fumana procumbens* and *Helianthemum oelandicum* are only found here, the former growing on both islands and the latter only on Öland.

For thousands of years, the islands' landscapes have been characterised by their ancient limestone plains, described by Carl Fries as a mixture of Asian steppe and Nordic fell. The similarities to the fells are apparent in the flora, which includes the red alpine chamion on Öland, and the white alpine butterwort and violet alpine bartsia. All three are typical upland

Sigsarve beach on north-west Gotland. Inside the steep cliffs lies the Hall-Hangvar nature reserve, nearly nine hundred hectares of sparse pine forest, smooth exposed rock and bogs. The beach is covered in polished limestone pebbles. The name Hall-Hangvar was given by sailors, and may have something to do with the hanging cliffs.

The lighthouse on the southernmost tip of Gotland was not built until 1846. It is a well-known seamark to thousands of contestants in the annual Gotland Runt regatta.

species and rather out of place in a coastal setting. Indeed, the limestone plains support many plants and flowers that only occur rarely, if at all, in other parts of Sweden. The globularia, for instance, grows no closer than Spain, while the small yellow-flowered shrubby cinquefoil bush is more at home in Siberia.

Equally, the fauna that inhabits the dry and warm limestone plateaus includes an array of uncommon species. The European green toad, a denizen of the steppes of Eastern Europe and Central Asia, occurred on Öland up until the 1980s, but sadly is no longer thought to survive on the island. The green toad is capable of surviving long periods of drought, as is the strange *Hielicopsis striata*, a species of snail that occurs only on Öland. Carl Fries once recalled how a group of snails that had spent 15 years in a collection deprived of food and water suddenly began crawling around when put on a bed of damp moss.

People have lived on Öland and Gotland ever since the islands emerged from the then Littorina Sea seven thousand years ago. The first inhabitants were hunters and fishermen. Explorations of the caves of Stora Karlsö, a small island just off the Gotland coast, have uncovered many axes, chisels, harpoons, fish hooks, pottery fragments, bone and horn from the early Stone Age.

Fishing was an important food source on both islands, and the latter half of the 19th century was an intensive period for the fishermen of Stora Karlsö and its smaller, adjoining cousin, Lilla Karlsö. Norderhamn harbour on Stora Karlsö had sixty fishing huts, though the fishermen did not live in them but in the caves, just like their Stone Age ancestors. The huts were where the men mended their nets and made fish hooks.

Not since the Stone Age has fishing been the dominant economic activity on Öland or Gotland. Nowadays, with cod and eel stocks under threat, there is precious little left for the fishermen to catch. Agriculture, especially sheep farming, has long been the main way of life. Gotland even has its own breed of sheep, the Gotland peltsheep, first established on the island by the Vikings, who brought back Karakul and Romanov breeds from Russian expeditions and crossed them with the native sheep.

Olaus Magnus, a prominent Swedish churchman and writer, wrote in 1555 in his *History of the Northern People*:

"In the Geatish (Baltic) Sea lies an island that comes under the Kingdom of Götaland, or Sweden, named Gotland, which means the good country, so called by all who doth visit it because it, more than other Nordic islands, can be esteemed and richly praised for its many natural gifts. The rams born here are stronger and statelier than others and hath four or eight horns... Their wool is long and soft, and when such wool hath been taken to Rome, as hath happened from time to time, and been

Keeping the livestock out: A cottage inside a thick stone wall, and a wall of its own for the pump. Öländska Alvaret near Vickleby.

Hoary rock-rose in Stora Alvaret, a limestone plain on Öland designated a World Heritage Site by UNESCO for its extraordinary biodiversity and prehistory.

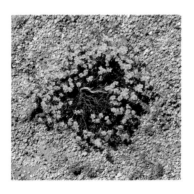

woven there into items of cloth, it hath been heartily praised by the beret makers there."

In Magnus's day, Gotland was actually under Danish control and did not become fully Swedish until the Treaty of Brömsebro in 1645. But the writer was accurate in his description of the status and importance of the Gotland sheep. These hardy creatures have played a central part in shaping Gotland's patchwork of heaths and pastures, as well as being of prime importance for merchant trade from the Iron Age to the early medieval era.

Gotland's mercantile history reflects its status as a trade and shipping centre. The island's soil is seemingly awash with old coins, gold jewellery, silverware and other valuables that were either buried or lost. No less than a quarter of all Viking coins found between the Ural Mountains and the River Elbe have been found by Gotland farmers while out ploughing their fields.

Strategically situated, located between the Russian city of Novgorod and Lübeck in northern Germany, the island was ideally positioned as a trading hub. Viking longships, cogs and other cargo vessels used Visby, Gotland's main city, as a Baltic hub. By the medieval era Visby was the richest metropolis in Scandinavia. But after reaching its peak in the twelfth and thirteenth centuries, Visby saw itself eclipsed during the 1300s as traders began to sail on other routes. The decline was completed when Danish King Valdemar Atterdag attacked and sacked the city in 1361, a trauma from which Visby did not really recover until the late twentieth century, when it became the East Coast summer and party town of choice.

Öland shares a similar, if somewhat less dramatic, historical trajectory. Here, too, agriculture and livestock farming were – and remain – key sources of income and employment. The island's steppe-like limestone plains are the product of centuries of grazing by sheep, horses and cattle. Livestock exports generated substantial revenue: records from the Prussian city of Danzig in 1476 detail the arrival of 30 ships from Öland carrying oxen and cattle, more than 500 horses, butter, cheese, meat, furs, hides, lambskins, fabrics, tallow, cod and herring.

Olaus Magnus was as impressed by Öland's riches as those of Gotland:

"Eland, or Öland, in the Geatish Sea is the most beautiful of islands, separated from Southern Götaland by a narrow sound. Such are its natural riches that its limited size (which one can cover in a two day journey) is compensated by the fertility of the soil. Meadows and fields beareth the scent of herbaceous plants and cultivate admiration for their indescribable delightfulness. There are considerable herds of small but sturdy horses, whose stamina and movement taketh precedence over many horses

An ancient sacrificial site located in the open area to the left gave its name to Visby, which became a powerful trading post in medieval times. The unusually well preserved walls and the entire city within are listed as a UNESCO World Heritage Site.

of stouter dimensions. Local and visiting merchants buy them for their amusement and to sell them as a superior creature."

Öland in Swedish takes its name literally from the word *ö*, meaning island. Contrary to what Olaus Magnus believed, Gotland's etymology comes not from "good country" (from the word *gott* for good) but from the Goths who lived there in around the first century.

Pollen data and fossilised remains tell us that both Öland and Gotland were largely covered by deciduous woodlands six or seven thousand years ago. The late poet, essayist and botanist Sten Selander tells us that these forests were damper, darker and more impenetrable than any we know today:

"We know that a primeval forest swathed the plains in a billowing blanket covering many tens of kilometres… We can also piece together details of the green chaos of this lost countryside. Ancient oaks were smothered by heavy, tangled clumps of ivy; bunches of mistletoe lay concealed in the tops of lime trees; and saplings sprouted from the ground, entangled with the undergrowth, where an old tree had fallen to the ground. Wild boar rummaged on the forest floor for acorns and roots."

Under these shady canopies Stone Age man sought prey with his flint weapons and primitive traps. These hunter-gatherers left only a light imprint on the land, but things changed when farming communities began to emerge. Vast areas of forest were thinned and felled to create fields and pasture. Sheep, horses, cattle and pigs nibbled off the shoots and saplings, creating a tamed, open landscape more reminiscent of the Mediterranean. And in common with countries like Greece, Italy and Spain, Öland and Gotland have also suffered the problems of erosion associated with overgrazing. Paradoxically, the main concern nowadays is not erosion but the disappearance of grazing animals.

Should you wish to gain an impression of what the ancient woodland landscape was like, the place to visit is Mittlandet on Öland, ideally the villages of Rönnerum and Abbantorp ten kilometres or so south of Borgholm, the major town on the island. The area has Sweden's largest continuous expanse of deciduous forest, which Selander described as "enormously lush groves of oak and hazel, interspersed with smooth-leafed elm and a diverse layer of most of the herbs and grasses found in mixed oak woodland, along with marshy stretches of ash, field elm and aspen".

In truth, this is no Stone Age forest but altogether younger woodland that has sprung up on abandoned pastures. This is what happens when grazing ceases and is a clear trend, not just on Öland and Gotland but on all the large archipelago islands – and across the entire country for that matter. UNESCO's decision in 2000 to classify southern Öland as a World Heritage Site was partly to preserve the open agricultural land-

Jordhamn in Persnäs parish on northern Öland. The skeleton of an old wind-powered polishing mill can still be seen here, remnant of a once-important limestone export industry. Women did the polishing, while the men sailed out and sold the finished product.

Ismantorp hill fortress on Öland, a defended settlement since the fourth century. Within the wall are outlines of buildings in an extraordinarily tight pattern: nine openings in the wall led to some 88 structures. More than a just defensive shield, it was a compact little city.

scape, the rich flower meadows and the unique limestone plateau, with its rock-roses, shrubby cinquefoils and bleating sheep.

Gotland nurtures similar ambitions, and nature conservancy organisations there are working hard to keep the meadows and heathlands open. It is tough battle. The face of agriculture is changing as farms are bought up by people from the mainland and divided up into summer-house plots. As the tourist hordes grow, so the sheep flocks diminish. Perhaps things will come full circle and the islands will revert to forest. One just hopes that people do not plant ill-conceived spruce plantations, but allow the land to revert to its true heritage of rich and diverse broad-leaf woodland.

The idyllic and nearly forgotten village of Bruddesta on the west coast of Öland. The fishing shacks are built of local limestone and the roofs are thatched. Some equipment remains, but the fishing is gone.

Närsholmen, a low, flat peninsula on south-east Gotland. This is a heavily grazed, savannah-like landscape with the occasional gnarled juniper and a smattering of pine trees (overleaf).

The Baltic thunders in on Själsö fishing village north of Visby. A summer storm can cause heavier seas than winter's harshest weather, as warm water moves more easily (previous pages).

Näsudden on south-west Gotland has the highest concentration of wind turbines in Sweden. The first power plant was opened here in 1983, and about one hundred turbines are in place today. Wind power on Gotland generates 170 million kilowatt-hours a year, some one-fifth of the island's total consumption.

The steep northern cliff on Stora Karlsö, with Lilla Karlsö in the background. Legend has it that on the evening of the 7th of August each year, the young guillemots jump into the water and leave the island, swimming.

Bredsands udde on Gotska Sandön, with shifting dunes and stabilising vegetation. In the background is a glimpse of Bredsand lighthouse, built in 1859. Gotska Sandön lies 38 kilometres north of Fårö, and is the most isolated spot in Sweden and the entire Baltic Sea. The island is the highest point in a fifty-kilometre reef stretching north from Fårö. Gotska Sandön was designated a national park in 1963 (previous pages).

Boy meets tree. Long exposure to wind makes this pine inviting to a climber. On the horizon lies Blå Jungfrun.

The Öland Bridge between
Kalmar and Färjestaden. At
more than six kilometres, the
bridge was Europe's longest
when it was inaugurated on
September 30, 1972. Island life
changed overnight, as tourists
flocked over during summer, but
more importantly as locals found
they could still live near family
and friends while commuting to
the mainland for work.

Eel traps in Kalmarsund, near Äleklinta on Öland. This area was fished from prehistoric times until the beginning of the twenty-first century, but a decline in eel populations has forced strict rationing of eel fishing permits.

The Långe Jan lighthouse on the southern tip of Öland. The highest in Sweden at 42 metres, Långe Jan was fuelled by coal when built in 1785, but is now all-electric and fully automatic. The area is also home to the Ottenby bird observatory, founded in 1946. In 2007, some 371 species were sighted here – a Swedish record (overleaf).

STOCKHOLM ARCHIPELAGO

Stockholm is home to the largest and most varied of Sweden's archipelagos, ranging from busy, forested islands overlooking the mainland to a vast network of islets and skerries further out to sea. Traditional industries have in recent years been supplemented by ecotourism and distance working via broadband connection, helping to reverse the depopulation tide. Many of the islands between Trosa and Gräsö are now expanding again.

The coastal waters outside Stockholm are home to Sweden's largest archipelago – a scattered patchwork of twenty-four thousand islands, islets and skerries. The most distant, the islands of Svenska Björn, Skarv and Svenska Högarna, lie some 80 kilometres from the city centre and the quaysides where thousands of people board ferries to visit the islands in summer time.

Lake Mälaren, around which Stockholm is built, was part of the Baltic Sea in the Middle Ages and the archipelago then stretched 150 kilometres inland. By the twelfth century, the land uplift caused by retreating glaciers following the last Ice Age had created an easterly outflow of water, and Lake Mälaren finally became separated from the sea.

Even today, the lake is barely a metre or so above sea level and surges in the Baltic occasionally reverse the eastward flow of water though Stockholm's sluices. If global warming leads to higher sea levels, as many people fear, then perhaps Lake Mälaren's islands will once again become conjoined with their salt-water cousins.

In this chapter we include the adjacent archipelagos of Oxelösund, Tystberga and Trosa, adding an additional thousand or so islands and skerries. Combined with the Stockholm archipelago, these form an island kingdom stretching 200 kilometres from north to south.

Stockholm is itself a child of the archipelago, built on islands straddling the confluence of fresh water and the brackish Baltic. But its large inner islands – Lidingö, Sicklaön, Orminge, Värmdö, Ingarö, Djurö and Vaxholm – are a world away from the windswept, mostly unspoilt outlying skerries. Shaped by decades of urban development and population growth, the inner islands have lost much of their original archipelago flavour. The vestiges that remain are confined to parks, recreation areas and reserves. Ekoparken in central Stockholm, the world's first national city park, and a few other enclaves have survived the relentless advance of concrete, and here you can still find small areas that support a typical archipelago flora.

For a taste of the true archipelago one must visit the Fjäderholmarna, a cluster of four small islands in Stockholm Bay 25 minutes by boat from the centre of town. The islands are home to the archipelago's largest

"Lommen's Shack" on the island of Gillöga was moved here in the mid-1800s by a fisherman named Johan Erik Österman. The moniker comes from Österman's son, who was nicknamed Lommen after a type of boat (p. 168).

The outer edge of the Söderarm archipelago, last stop before the Åland Sea. Generations of sailors have waited here for the right weather and wind to cross to the Åland islands (pp. 170–171).

Evening sun over a harbour in Vaxholm. In the background is a glimpse of the old stone fortress on Rindö. The first tower was built by King Gustav Vasa in 1548, and the current structure dates back to the 1840s. Vaxholm is the hub for boat traffic, and sailors consider it a gateway to the archipelago. But the tiny City of Vaxholm also faces Stockholm, and many of the 6,000 residents within the municipality commute to work in the big city to the west (previous pages).

The innermost islands of the Stockholm Archipelago. At the bottom is Blasieholmen. In the centre is Skeppsholmen, which hosts the city's Modern Art Museum and East Asian Museum. Across the water a Viking Line ship leaves harbour and heads out into the archipelago on a cruise, likely to Finland or Åland.

colony of lesser black-backed gulls and, more oddly, a population of barnacle geese, an Arctic species that in recent years has started to breed at a few habitats throughout the Baltic. The bird life, flora and way of life on Fjäderholmarna are considered so characteristic of the archipelago that Swedish national television company, SVT, in the 1980s chose the islands as the film location for its "Öbergs på Lillöga" TV drama series about archipelago life.

If, though, you want to see the archipelago countryside as it looked in bygone days you should head for Bogesundslandet, at one time an island but now joined to the mainland. Thanks to the presence of a large privately owned estate, it has managed to keep property speculators and urban planners at bay. Twentieth century Swedish zoologist and author Carl Fries described Bogesundslandet as "a large swath of ancient Sweden on Stockholm's doorstep" and was fond of exploring the area:

"The most wonderful woodland meadows lie concealed among groves and leafy dells. Here, bumble bees buzz over the cow clover, and bluebells and laserworts raise their white parasols skywards deep beneath the shady oak canopy. The full wealth of Sweden's floral beauty is on show as spring and summer unfold…

"For miles the beach stretches along Askrikefjärden and Stora Värtan, with not a house in sight. Just across the water lie Lidingö and Djursholm, where built-up areas sprout everywhere amongst the greenery. To the east, the main sailing channel stretches for ten kilometres past strips of coast spotted with houses. Only Bogesundslandet stands free and uncluttered, like a giant postscript in our modern-day archipelago of summer houses and cottages."

The seeming paradox of a powerful landowner keeping developers in check is by no means unique to Bogesundslandet. The coastline of Sörmland, the county immediately south of Stockholm, is dominated by large estates where powerful landowners have also maintained an iron grip. Their unwillingness to sell their land has largely saved the archipelagos of Oxelösund and Trosa from being divided up into summer house plots. Centuries ago, the landowners also wielded similarly tight control over fishing rights. As a result, there are few fishing communities here compared to other parts of coastal Sweden. Indeed, until a hundred years ago more people in Sörmland earned their livelihoods from freshwater fishing than sea fishing. Instead, arable and livestock farming – the time-honoured mainstays of the estates – dominated the coastline (and still do on many of the larger islands).

The largest island on the Sörmland coast, Ringsö, came close to breaking the mould in the 1950s when its owner was petitioned to build 300 summer cottages on his property. But in the end he declined the offer, and Ringsö remains open to walkers, bathers and beachcombers.

Rain-laden skies and patches of glistening sun in the outer archipelago. Here at the edge of the open sea, the islands are low, barren and widely spaced.

A curious grey seal near Svenska Björn, situated at the rim of Stockholm archipelago.

Local nature reserves have been set up in many areas to protect the unspoilt environment. The coast is also highly popular with marine biologists, with the island of Askö, just offshore from the picturesque town of Trosa, hosting the largest marine research laboratory on Sweden's east coast. The location was specifically chosen for its clean waters, and the laboratory was built in 1961 to explore the workings of an unspoilt marine ecosystem.

Things did not work out quite as planned, though. Soon after the lab opened came reports of disruption to the Baltic marine environment. Researchers discovered that areas of oxygen-deprived sea bottom were spreading at an alarming rate as water visibility declined. These first signs of eutrophication – enrichment by chemical nutrients – prompted Askö's scientists to focus instead on monitoring the changes in the ecosystem.

When I landed at Askö one July day in 1973, a lush reedbed growing by the jetty caught my eye. "Oh yes," said laboratory manager Bengt-Owe Jansson when I asked him about it, "that's where the waste water from our kitchen and toilet runs into the sea." The lab lacked enough money to build a proper water treatment plant, but at least it enabled the scientists to study pollution at close hand.

It was this type of effluent – nitrates from toilets and kitchens and phosphates from detergents – that worried the researchers most. The effects were already there to see in the form of green carpets of blanketweed algae in the water. It was at Askö that I made my first acquaintance with this thread-like species that clung to jetties and rocks and choked the naturally occurring kelp seaweed.

Nutrient-rich waters are a haven for the fast-growing blanketweed algae. It can attach itself to kelp and other longer-lived algae, sometimes forming carpets so thick as to deprive the host plant of all light. This alters the ecosystem, and the blanketweed takes over. Blanketweed is now the most familiar algae species in the Baltic Sea. Meanwhile, kelp has retreated from many of its former haunts. Between the 1930s and 1990s, around half the kelp in the Stockholm archipelago disappeared, which can be described only as a disaster. Kelp, which belongs to the brown algae, grows in dense underwater clusters that offer food and protection to animal plankton and young and small fish. The sandhoppers and Baltic isopods which thrive in kelp forests are the staple food of many fish species.

But all is not doom and gloom. Around 15 years ago, scientists detected the first signs of a recovery. The sea was a fraction less murky and nutrient levels slightly lower. On a drizzly July day in 2001, I met up with marine biologist Lena Kautsky, Bengt-Owe Jansson's successor at the Askö laboratory. She and her assistants were planting bunches of kelp

View from the guest-house owned by the Archipelago Foundation on Långviksskär. The house once belonged to American Ambassador William W. Thomas, who came here in the 1890s and over time bought most of the island and its surrounding skerries. The artist and author Axel Sjöberg frequented the island, and for many years the Archipelago Foundation has awarded an annual grant in his name allowing two artists to spend five weeks in Ambassador Thomas's house.

Örskär is one of a small number of lighthouse stations established in the seventeenth century. The present tower, from 1740, is by Carl Hårleman who also designed the Royal Palace in Stockholm.

among the rocks in the water to see if the seaweed would return when the marine environment improved. When I spoke to Lena a few years later, she confirmed the positive trend and even said the kelp was beginning to recolonise the seabed.

Public attention in the last decade or so has focused on the huge summertime blooms of poisonous algae, and here excess nutrients seem not to be the main villain. The summer of 2005 saw the worst algal bloom in history, with a thick, toxic asparagus-coloured soup floating in the sea. A few months earlier, the governmental environmental protection committee had warned that the Baltic was caught in a eutrophication cycle and dying a slow death. The toxic algal bloom was just an unpleasant confirmation of this trend, the committee said.

But years of scientific data gathered from the Stockholm archipelago were at odds with the committee's findings. There, the water was getting clearer and less polluted by nutrients. There had to be another explanation.

Heat is clearly a factor, since algae require warmth to bloom successfully. The summers of the 21st century have been favourable in that regard, possibly due to global warming. Another factor is phosphorous, which occurs naturally in deep-sea sediment. Inflows of salt water to the Baltic during westerly gales apparently disturb phosphorous deposits, releasing them into the water.

So algal blooms may be a natural phenomenon, at least in part. Perhaps they used to occur in the warm waters of the Littorina Sea, ancestor of the Baltic, thousands of years before humans started flushing toilets and washing with detergents.

Overfishing of cod has also been cited as a contributory factor. The Swedish Board of Fisheries says the sharp decline in cod stocks has disrupted the food chain all the way down to the algae and toxic cyanobacteria that cause algal blooms. The disappearance of cod has benefited sprats, which eat a diverse array of marine crustaceans, fish larvae and other organisms, so paving the way for algae to multiply and bloom successfully.

The fisheries board has proposed introducing large sprat quotas to restore the ecological balance, though the strategy of seeking to right one wrong with a second wrong shows just how difficult and complex a task it is to keep the Baltic Sea alive and healthy.

Between the large, built-up islands of the inner archipelago and the small outer skerries lies a band of medium-sized islands – Utö, Ornö, Nämdö, Runmarö and Möja – that can be described as the heart of the Stockholm archipelago. The communities here are large enough to be self-sustaining, and though the old industries of livestock farming and eel, herring and cod fishing are of marginal importance nowadays,

Furusund in the foreground and Köpmanholmen behind – near where the iconic Swedish playwright August Strindberg lived and where he placed the action – under other names – in *A Dream Play*. Children's author Astrid Lindgren also had a summer home here which is said to have inspired her charming *Seacrow Island* about an inept city family summering in the isolated community and the friends who help them understand local ways.

a sense of modern optimism is noticeable among the villagers. Modern communications technology has given them and their communities a new lease of life.

Once plagued by depopulation, the islands have seen their populations grow in the last thirty years, a trend unique in any of Sweden's archipelagos (if you exclude the large islands close to urban centres and with permanent connections to the mainland).

Utö's population has tripled since the 1960s to almost 240 people today, while Ornö has grown from 133 residents in 1971 to around 250. Runmarö, one of the most expansive islands, boasts its own school, marina, boatyard, pub, shop, mechanic's and even a sailmaker's. Two hundred and eighty-five people live there and their number swells tenfold during the popular summer season.

More people are also moving out to some of the larger islands close to the mainland. Ljusterö, one of the largest, now has more than 1,500 year-round residents, double the number in the 1960s. Tynningö, Rindö, Skarpö, Yxlan, Blidö, Arholma and Gräsö are also growing.

The islands off Stockholm are without doubt the subject of more songs and writing than any of Sweden's archipelagos. Luminaries like the eighteenth century poet and musician Carl Michael Bellman and singer-songwriter-author Evert Taube, who died in 1976, drew much inspiration from the area. Another was author and playwright August Strindberg, whose 1887 novel *The Natives of Hemsö* was about the life of people on the fictional island Hemsö, modelled on the real island of Kymmendö, where Strindberg spent part of his youth. The contents of the book so infuriated Kymmendö's inhabitants that Strindberg was never able to set foot there again.

In his stead, other writers followed in Strindberg's footsteps on Kymmendö. In 1941, the poet and essayist Werner Aspenström was despatched there by the national employment agency to work in a children's summer camp. So charmed was he by the island that he returned every summer for the next 50 years and wrote a book, *Summer*, about life in Strindberg's former haunts.

Forced to forsake Kymmendö, Strindberg spent his summers on Runmarö, where he wrote the psychological thriller *By the Open Sea*. The book tells the story of a government fisheries inspector who arrives on a small island named Österskär. Österskär was also an imaginary place but closely modelled on Huvudskär, one of the remotest island outposts. From Huvudskär, a series of islets, skerries and rocky outcrops stretches north to the island of Söderarm, forming the wildest and most dramatic part of the archipelago.

A journey into these parts is a bit like being in the Swedish fells. You travel through similar landscapes – from the coniferous woodland of the

The sheltered harbour of Kyrkviken on the island of Möja. This is one of the oldest and liveliest communities in the Stockholm archipelago. About 230 people live permanently on the island, a number that has scarcely changed in decades. Bountiful fishing and thriving strawberry farms provided income in the past; now ecotourism and broadband Internet are more important. There are almost no cars on the island, but any number of three-wheeled mopeds for transportation and deliveries.

central archipelago, via the birch-clad outlying islands, to the smooth bare rock surfaces of the outermost skerries. The environment is harsher, but also richer. The islets and just-visible reefs are thousands of years old and have a surprisingly long economic history, too. Looking at a cluster of islands named Skarv on an old nautical chart from 1805, the words "Fishing cottages" appear marked on the largest island.

The late archipelago author Sten Rinaldo wrote in his book *Vägen till Skarv* (The Way to Skarv) that the islands were inhabited by fishermen as long ago as the sixteenth century. They lived "on rounded slabs of rock in the sea, which were almost submerged by the swell in south-easterly gales". The fishermen carved labyrinths and compass cards on the rocks, and in 1572 paid fish as tax to the Crown. Rinaldo wrote:

"The tiny house on Skarv island is a place like no other along Sweden's coast. Rocks in the sea that tell an old, unique story and which to this very day bear witness to where it all began – the Earth's creation."

A channel buoy, one of thousands in the Stockholm archipelago.

The sailing yacht *Solbris* anchors for the night near Gillöga.

A red Viking Line ship meets a white Silja Line vessel at Stockholm's Frihamnen harbour. To the right is the suburban residential island of Lidingö, and far across the water in the rear is the outline of the Royal Palace in the Old Town (overleaf).

Söderöra is a genuine fishing hamlet with a strong boat-building tradition that has remained largely unchanged since the end of the eighteenth century. Twenty people live here all year round and four hundred over the summer months. (pp. 188–189).

The Björnö peninsula on Ingarö is a nature reserve managed by the Archipelago Foundation. Agriculture on Björnö can be dated back to the Iron Age.

Archipelago Boat Day is celebrated every summer on the first Wednesday in June. The event assembles a flotilla including old passenger ferries like the *Västan*, built in 1900, as well as modern vessels such as the *Sandhamn* powered by waterjet propulsion. Boats are essential to the economic vitality of the archipelago, transporting 1.8 million passengers a year (overleaf).

Stora Alskär is a popular daytrip destination, with no permanent residences but with sheets of well-polished rock from which to wade into the sea. Vegetation is rich here, with wild fruit trees indicating that people once lived on the island (pp. 194–195).

The lighthouse on Söderarm was built in 1838 and was manned until 1997, when the last lighthouse keeper, Ivan Wallin, moved to a home on the mainland. During the Cold War, military facilities were housed in chambers blasted in the rock under the lighthouse. These are now permanently sealed.

The Tjärven lighthouse northwest of Söderarm is in a remote and exposed position, but within view of more protected islands. Built in 1902, the original structure looked like a medieval castle, but restoration in the 1950s smoothed out the contours. On a rock below the tower a homesick lighthouse keeper has carved "Island of Loneliness".

Piers, boathouses and red cabins on Möja. Earlier residents preferred to find leeward spots to build their houses, but summer residents – who have been arriving in a steady stream since steamboat traffic began in the early 1900s – build higher to take advantage of sea views (previous pages).

Wildflowers and herbs growing on Svenska Högarna, a distant archipelago outpost and a popular sailing destination in calm weather. Once an important fishing harbour, Svenska Högarna is now one of Sweden's most attractive workplaces, with employers including the Swedish Meteorological and Hydrological Institute, the Environmental Protection Agency and the Archipelago Foundation.

Sandhamn, one of the best-known islands in the Stockholm archipelago, is home to about 120 permanent residents and some 3,000 summer visitors. Some moor here in pleasure boats, while others arrive on ferries and stay in hotels (previous pages).

Bathing from the cliffs near Sandhamn. The water seldom gets above 20°C, but to slip into the cool water from a sun-heated rock is singular pleasure.

A canoeist passes Norsten in the outer archipelago. The island is known as a birdwatcher's paradise, and for two labyrinths – one an exact copy of a design from a 3,000-year-old shard of Greek pottery.

Ålandsskär, where fishermen have kept their boats since the Middle Ages. The original harbour was founded by King Karl Knutsson in 1450, and by the early 1600s there were sixteen boathouses around the group of islets. These were all burned during the Russian invasion of 1719, but by 1900 a thriving community included pilots, lighthouse keepers and enough children to warrant a school. By the 1970s all the permanent residents had moved away, and the old Customs House serves today as a summer youth hostel (previous pages).

Heavy seas roll in to Horsten, east of Sandhamn. This was the main archipelago fishing outpost from the Middle Ages until the early 1800s, supporting a chapel, a cemetery and perhaps a hundred shacks.

Hallskär, south-east of Bullerö, is a sailor's paradox – you can enjoy the silence among the outer skerries, which is safe as well as adventurous.

NORTH COAST

With its deep forests, steep cliffs and stony beaches, this is the most untamed of Sweden's coastlines. It is also the most industrialised, with large towns and thriving business communities. The archipelago stretching from Gävle to Haparanda is narrow and thinly populated, though some of the larger islands do support year-round communities.

The North Coast is long and stretches from the Bay of Gävle to the Torne River at the very top of the Baltic Sea. It is a landscape of dense pine forest, wood processing factories and river estuaries.

The coastal islands, typically dotted with coniferous forest and rowan trees, are widely scattered. Apart from in the inner reaches of the Gulf of Bothnia, the North Coast lacks major archipelagos like the ones further south.

Industrial forestry is omnipresent along the coast. Pulp and paper plants cluster around the mouths of large rivers, where in bygone days the logs would end their journey after being floated downstream. (These days, the timber arrives by truck.) Forestry played a pioneering role in bringing industrialisation to these northern climes, and though mechanisation means that relatively few people are employed to work in the forests and factories nowadays, forestry retains a strong social and cultural imprint.

Forestry has also left its mark on the environment – literally. In some areas, such as the Bay of Gävle, the seabed is heavily contaminated with toxins. Here, the pulp factories of Skutskär, Korsnäs, Norrsundet, Vallvik and Iggesund spewed vast amounts of chlorine and other chemicals straight into the sea for decades. It was only a matter of time before scientists would start to sound the alarm bells, and by the 1980s fish were dying in their thousands and showing signs of physical defects. The marine environment was in crisis.

The forestry companies responded by installing water treatment plants and adapting their production processes to reduce effluent. The Korsnäs pulp and paper complex, one of the worst polluters, introduced new methods to bleach pulp using oxygen and other less harmful chemicals. The company built a new production line and switched from debarking logs using water to doing it dry, a move that stopped anaerobic and other harmful chemicals from being released into the water.

The benefits were not slow in coming. Kelp, a key barometer of a healthy marine environment, staged a comeback and biologists observed a recovery in fish reproduction. Water clarity improved and new layers of

Högbonden lighthouse, Ångermanland. Right at the top of Högbonden island, 60 metres above sea level, is a lighthouse station built in 1909. At most, 21 people lived here. The lighthouse was automated in 1963, and in the 80s the building was turned into a youth hostel (p. 210).

The high pylons of the Höga kusten Bridge stick up through the clouds. The new suspension bridge across Ångermanälven is 1,800 metres long and the pylons are 180 metres tall – making the bridge one of the tallest structures in Sweden (pp. 212–213).

The view across Ullångersfjärden from the hamlet of Salsåker on Höga kusten (previous pages).

Ulvöhamn on the northern part of Ulvön island in Ångermanland. This is the worldwide Mecca for lovers of fermented herring. At the end of the nineteenth century, people first began to put yeast and salted herring into sealed tin cans. Today, 50 people live year round on Ulvön.

sediment began forming and covering over the sins of the past. We must now pin our hopes on the seabed being left undisturbed so the heavy metals and other pollutants remain encased in the sediment.

When zoologist Carl Fries explored the Gulf of Bothnia by boat in the 1930s, he proposed Herring Coast as a new name for Sweden's shores, reasoning that "the Gold Coast, the Slave Coast and the Ivory Coast inherited their names from their most precious products. By the same token, the Swedish coast, a rich source of herring, could be called the Herring Coast."

Herring fishing has historically played a vital economic role for communities the length and breadth of Sweden's Baltic coast, particularly the northern section between Gävle and the Gulf of Bothnia. Its importance dates back to medieval times, when people learned the art of seine fishing and making nets with small enough meshes to catch herring. The industry had its centre in Gävle, which benefited from a decree signed by King Gustav Vasa in 1557 giving the city's fishermen the right to fish for herring along the entire North Coast in return for delivering every tenth barrel of salted herring to the Crown.

During the summer months, Gävle s fishermen rowed their boats along the coast as far north as Ångermanland province, calling in at fifty or so fishing harbours on the way. Their catches earned them large sums of money and were the foundation of the city's prosperity. A memorandum written in 1621 to Kristina, dowager queen and consort to King Karl IX, stated that three quarters of Gävle's townspeople were fishermen and the rest were merchants. Herring supplies were plentiful in those days and records show that 6,500 barrels were landed in Gävle harbour in 1742, rising to 10,000 barrels in 1816.

The barrels were sold to neighbouring provinces and counties or bartered for corn. They were in great demand: salted herring was a staple of people's daily diet across eastern Sweden until well into the eighteenth century, and it is estimated that the average household ate a quarter of a barrel per year. By that measure, the Gävle fishermen's catch in 1816 would have been enough to feed forty thousand people for twelve months. By the early 1900s, the advent of modern transport in the form of cars and motorised boats saw people switch to tastier fresh herring from the salted variety.

For the moment, herring stocks remain plentiful. But overfishing is a long-term threat, and you can be sure that prices will rise if numbers fall. Then, perhaps, herring will finally be seen not as a staple commodity but as the delicacy it truly is.

For centuries a community-based industry, herring fishing is now almost entirely dominated by large trawlers. The main fishing grounds are in the central Baltic, off the island of Gotland, and in the Gulf of Bothnia, the

Fishermen empty their salmon fishing nets in Luleå archipelago. Salmon fishing has always been an important form of livelihood in the Gulf of Bothnia, but the catches have become much smaller in recent decades, down from 400 tonnes in 1990 to 150 tonnes in 2006. Overfishing, low rates of breeding adults returning upstream, and the mysterious disease called M 74 are some explanations for the reduction.

upper arm of the Baltic running north from the Åland islands. Here, Finnish fleets account for more than ninety per cent of the catch and the industry in Sweden has dwindled to a mere fraction of what it was in its heyday.

So, the name Herring Coast is redundant these days, and more tourist-friendly names like the Virgin Coast and the High Coast are in vogue instead. The Virgin Coast runs from the Bay of Gävle to the Hornslandet peninsula outside Hudiksvall and is named after the island of Storjungfrun (meaning Virgin) and its lighthouse. Though the origins of the name are unclear, the island was called Helgön or Heligön (Holy Island) until the seventeenth century, so presumably there was indeed a connection to the Virgin Mary.

The Virgin Coast is shallow and stony, its islands widely scattered. Only between Axmarsfjärden Bay in the south and Hudiksvallsfjärden Bay in the north do you find anything like an archipelago – a twenty kilometre string of 500 or so islands and islets.

Few people live out here. Only four islands between Gävle and Sundsvall – a distance of more than two hundred kilometres – have full time residents, and between them they have a grand total of twelve inhabitants. Down the ages, even relatively large and well known islands like Prästgrundet, Agön, Enskär and Storjungfrun were inhabited only during the fishing season. When winter came, the fishing communities moved back to the mainland.

By contrast, several large islands on the High Coast north of Härnösand have sizeable resident communities. Hemsön and Ulvön, for instance, still have small scale herring industries and specialise in producing *surströmming*. This soured, or fermented, Baltic herring is considered a delicacy in Sweden and is typically consumed at special parties held during autumn, when it is washed down with liberal quantities of aquavit.

Ulvön was once one of the most important fishing harbours on the North Coast. First used as a summer fishing base by people from Gävle, it became home to a community of fishermen and farmers in the mid-sixteenth century. A chapel, built in 1622, still stands to this day. Towards the end of the nineteenth century, the island became renowned for its *surströmming* and later invented a technique for fermenting the herring in tin cans instead of wooden barrels, as had previously been the norm. The innovation quickly caught on, becoming a big export success, for the island. Though Ulvön s largest salting house closed down in 1982, when its packaging operations were relocated to the mainland, a few small salt houses still remain active.

The name High Coast, first coined in the 1970s, serves as a highly appropriate description for an area famed for its tall cliff formations.

The coast at Långsand where the Dalälven river enters Gävlebukten bay. The bedrock is visible here; otherwise the area is known for its sand and moraine. Close by is Billudden, a long arm of moraine that forms the end of the Uppsala ridge.

The Caspian Tern, the world's largest species of tern, is recognisable by its raucous croak and glowing red beak.

It is indeed the tallest area of coastline in Sweden and is still gaining height as the land continues its post-glacial elevation. A major High Coast landmark is Mjältön, which at two hundred and thirty-six metres above sea level is Sweden's highest island. Skuleberget Hill is another; a mere boulder in the sea ten thousand years ago, it is now a peak of two hundred and eighty-six metres.

The High Coast is currently rising at an annual rate of eight milli-metres, which is sufficiently fast for people in places like Nordingrå, Mjällom and Docksta to experience noticeable changes to the lie of the land during their lives. So strong is the uplift that many sixteenth century fishing harbours now stand marooned on land, cut off from their mari-time heritage. A modern-day harbour like Häggvik will in three hundred years' time no longer be beside the sea but will overlook an inland lake.

The High Coast's unique rapakivi granite formations (*rapakivi* is Finnish for "crumbly rock") saw it awarded a place on UNESCO's World Heritage List in 2000. In its official citation, UNESCO said the area "affords outstanding opportunities for the understanding of the important processes that formed the glaciated and land uplift areas of the Earth's surface."

Immediately north of the High Coast lies the low-lying and shallow Kvarken archipelago. Here the Gulf of Bothnia is at its narrowest, and the historical Finnish city of Vaasa is just eighty kilometres away across the water. The sea between the two countries is no deeper than thirty metres at this point and getting shallower by the year as the land eleva-tion continues. At the present rate, it will be possible to walk between the two countries in three thousand five hundred years' time.

As on the High Coast, land uplift has played a dominant role in sculpt-ing the Kvarken landscape. New islands rise from the sea and shipping channels become steadily shallower. The Kvarken archipelago, most of whose islands are in Finnish waters, is said to be growing at a rate of one hundred hectares a year. In 2006, UNESCO recognised this unusual geological phenomenon by inscribing the area on its World Heritage List as Kvarken Archipelago/High Coast.

In the heart of Kvarken lies the island of Holmön, once home to a colony of seal hunters and also noted for its excellent salmon fishing. Inhabited for 600 years, its societies were based on a strict division of labour between the men, who fished and hunted, and the women, who farmed the land and tended livestock. This social fabric still held sway in April 1939 when Carl Fries visited to accompany the hunters in their pursuit of grey and ringed seals. Fries recalled following the men across the ice on kick-sleds and described the island as "a singular place, this Swedish outpost in Kvarken: one long giant reef of rocks and pebbles arranged in terraces like staircases rising up to the highest point."

The lighthouse on Stora Fjäderägg north of Holmön island off Umeå. Residents of Holmön skied out here on the ice to hunt seals in the mid-twentieth century. Today, there is a frequently visited ornithological station and a youth hostel on the island. The entire area is part of the Holmö islands' large nature reserve.

The silhouette of Skuleskogen forest emerges from the sea like a dark swell in the moonlight. In this part of the Baltic the sea is deeper and the islands higher than anywhere else.

Out on the ice, Fries witnessed Holmön's top marksman despatch a ringed seal with a single rifle shot. "The seal lifts its head and gazes round. The opportunity is at hand and the marksman fires. It takes a few seconds before the shot is heard, but the seal has already slumped listlessly to the ice, killed instantaneously. There is great rejoicing."

Fries returned to Holmön two months later, this time to watch the salmon fishermen in action. "According to custom," he wrote, "all salmon fishing on Holmön is the privilege of the land-owning residents. It is organised on the lines of an old village householders' association… Like the eel fishing at Harstena, it is divided into lots that the villagers swap amongst themselves each year to make sure that no one hogs the best fishing spots."

Fries watched the men emptying their nets. Though only a single salmon had fastened in the mesh, it was a fine specimen weighing in at twelve kilograms, and it was sold for the eye-watering price of two hundred kronor per kilo. No wonder that salmon fishing was the favourite topic of conversation among the men of the village!

Nowadays there are no seal hunters or salmon fishermen on Holmön – and no women work in the fields. The centuries-old traditions that Fries described just seventy years ago are entirely gone.

The eastern part of Holmön is now a nature reserve and the adjacent island of Stora Fjäderägg is a bird observatory. Eighty people still live on the island, struggling to find new, innovative ways of earning a living. There is a school, a kindergarten, an old people's home, a shop and pub. An impressive looking website – www.holmon.com – does its bit to keep Holmön on the map.

At the top of the North Coast, in the inner reaches of the Gulf of Bothnia, an extensive network of close to three thousand islands and skerries provides a stark contrast to the spectacular cliffs of the High Coast. These low-lying, sandy islands are rarely higher than twenty metres and differ from all other Swedish archipelagos by having no bedrock, flat rocks or precipices. Built entirely of sand and moraine, they look more like Pacific atolls with their inviting sandy beaches and inlets.

Sten Selander, a writer and former Swedish Academy member until his death in 1957, once wrote of these parts: "With its long gravel ridges, low sandy islets and grey alder and sea buckthorn fringing pillar-shaped pines, the archipelago between Luleå and Haparanda is one of our strangest coastlines… The contours of this island kingdom, surrounded by the unremitting summertime light, are rougher than we are used to elsewhere. The whole atmosphere has an unfamiliar chill, telling us that the tundra and Arctic ice are not far away."

Common guillemots swarm around Bonden lighthouse in Norra Kvarken. About 700 pairs nest on this desolate red granite cliff out in the sea – it is ten kilometres to the nearest island. This is the second-largest colony of these birds in Sweden, after that on the Karlsö islands off Gotland.

The SCA pulp mill outside Sundsvall. These distinctive silhouettes are in many ways typical of the northern Sweden coastline.

Byske seaside resort, 30 kilometres north of Skellefteå, with its sandy beach, cottages, campsite, minigolf – and the salmon-rich Byskeälven river just around the corner.

The old Rönnskär fishing station in the Söderhamn archipelago. This is one of at least four Rönnskär (rowan skerry) islands along the northern Swedish coast, five if we include one on the Finnish side of the Gulf of Bothnia. Outside Skellefteå is the well-known Rönnskär where the Rönnskärsverken smelting plant is situated; by Piteå is Pite Rönnskär, by Stocka in Nordanstig municipality is another Rönnskär, and off Porkala peninsula in Kyrkslätt in Finland is an old lighthouse station called Rönnskär (overleaf).

The cottages, fishing shacks and jetties are well-kept at Kuggören on the North Coast, but due to land elevation the water depth in the harbour is now less than one metre. Further inland is a 1,340-metre-long, ten-thousand-year-old cave system – the second longest in Europe (p. 230–231).

Hölickskär lighthouse south-east
of Hudiksvall is from 1932.

A sandy beach with sea milk-wort and rubble-stones on the Hornslandet coast. A 750-year-old pine, Sweden's oldest, grows nearby.

233

Skuleskogen national park in Ångermanland. The picture was taken just above the mighty Slåttdalsskrevan rift, a 40-metre-deep, 7-metre-wide and 200-metre-long crevice in Skuleberget hill. The red rapakivi granite cracks easily, and the national park was created in 1984 specifically to preserve the steeply sloping landscape of flat rocky ground and rift valleys (previous pages).

A flowery meadow featuring crane's bill, buttercups and wild chervil in Mädan parish near Nordingrå on the High Coast.

Eider ducks in the southern Gulf of Bothnia off Umeå. The eider is Sweden's largest sea duck and is typical of the outer archipelago: it nests along the northern Swedish coast all the way up to Luleå archipelago. For several decades at the beginning of the twentieth century the eider was hunted so much that it almost became extinct along some areas of the coast. After the spring hunt was banned in the 1950s the eider population increased tenfold in only a few decades, and today there are perhaps 300,000 nesting pairs in Sweden.

Häggvik on Höga kusten in Ångermanland. The picture was taken from the Stortorget hill in Nordingrå, with a fine view across Gaviksfjärden and the steepsided islands (overleaf).

A promontory at the mouth of
the Torneälv river. Sand dunes
create wave patterns in the
water and build up a golden
sandbank along the green-clad
headland.

A tanker at the oil port in Luleå. 95 per cent of Sweden's export trade goes by sea.

Bergudden lighthouse on Holmön island off Umeå. The lighthouse was built in 1896 and is located on the western side of the island in order to cover Västra Kvarken. Originally, there was also a warning bell in the tower but this was later moved to the bell-tower of Holmön church. There are four lighthouses around the Holmö islands, and the Swedish Maritime Administration wants to shut them all down – something that has provoked strong public reaction, as usual when a lighthouse is threatened with closure. There is extremely strong public support for Swedish lighthouses. In 1996 the Swedish Lighthouse Society was formed to promote interest in the coastal lighthouses and help preserve them. The society now has more than 3,000 members.

Bjuröklubb off Lövånger in Västerbotten. The name means "beaver island club" and the shape resembles the club-like tail of a beaver. The lighthouse and lighthouse keeper's cottage were built in 1859 on the site of an old beacon. The lighthouse was automated and the personnel removed in 1970. The entire area became a nature reserve in 1995 to protect a beautiful example of the distinctive landscape and culture of the Västerbotten coast.

Haparanda Sandskär is the largest island in the Haparanda archipelago national park. The park was created in 1995 to preserve a fairly unspoiled area of this unique island world. The islands here are not made of bedrock, but were created out of sand and gravel. They also have a very low profile: 2,000 years ago this archipelago did not exist – it had not yet risen from the sea. Haparanda is not only at the northernmost point of the Swedish coastline; the town is also at the most easterly position – on the same longitude as Riga in Latvia (overleaf).

WINTER COAST

Winter in the archipelago is often windy and raw, with a shut-down, dormant feel. But it can sparkle crisp and bright in the snow and ice, too. The West Coast is generally ice-free, but further north, in the Gulf of Bothnia, the sea freezes every winter. Sometimes the ice is thick enough for people to reach the mainland by foot or snowmobile. But when it gets too thick the boats can no longer get through and the island communities become marooned again.

Winter evening near Hamburgön.
A thin layer of ice surrounds the
islet and a light snow whitens
the cliffs – an unusual sight
on Sweden's West Coast. The
Gulf Stream normally keeps the
waters open here, and winters
tend to be more grey than white
(p. 248).

Late winter on Rörö in the
Gothenburg archipelago. Nearly
three hundred people reside
year-round in the fishing village
here, with most still making their
living from the sea (previous
pages).

The old fishing village of Fykan
in Bohuslän, now reduced to a
few white homes and red boathouses. Summertime sees a brief
but intense influx of tourists, but
during winter the islands are
lashed by storms and boats are
tied up safely out of the water.

Boathouses in Björholmen, a tiny
fishing village founded in the
sixteenth century when herring
fishing was at its peak. The cliffs
are a perfect place to watch sail-
boats compete in the local regatta (previous pages).

Gothenburg and Lilla Bommens
Harbour, where the four-masted
Viking is permanently moored –
refitted as a hotel. To the west of
the four-masted bark lies the new
opera house, and by the bridge
is Ralph Erskine's crooked skyscraper, built in 1989.

257

Hovs Hallar nature reserve on the tip of the Bjäre peninsula in the county of Skåne. This is Sweden's mildest climate zone, and winters are often green and rainy. But when the seawater falls just below the freezing point and the air snaps even colder, a harbour can turn into an ice sculpture garden.

Street lamp and pollard transformed into ice sculptures in Kåseberga harbour on the south coast of Skåne.

North-eastern Skåne county. On the horizon under the struggling sun is Rakön, and to the right is Tosteberga, a narrow outcropping popular among birdwatchers. This is the place to sight white-tailed eagles, especially during the winter when local people leave out carrion for the majestic predators to feed upon when hunting is lean.

Äleklinta, an old fishing hamlet on the west coast of Öland, features a well-known bathing beach and views admired by artists for generations. There are no tracks in the snow at this time of year, but the nets hanging to dry attest to the usual activity here (overleaf).

Winter fog on north Öland
softens the snow-dusted slate
and naked bushes. The area
is known for steep cliffs and,
in clear weather, breathtaking
views over the Kalmarsund
waterway.

The locals still call these "Hahn's shacks" for the fisherman who held the rights to eel fishing here in the 1940s and '50s, Valfrid Hahn. The nearby birdwatching station is busy all year round, and even in January one will see a variety of seabirds and perhaps a white-tailed eagle on the hunt.

Visby, the largest town on the island of Gotland, slips into a different costume in winter. In the background lie the ruins of St. Karin's Church, sanctified in 1388. Of sixteen medieval churches in Visby, services are now held only in the thirteenth-century Maria Cathedral. Concerts and plays are staged in the ruins during summer.

Trosa River flows gently through the town that gave its name to a small and relatively untouched archipelago. "Welcome to Trosa – the end of the world", it says on a sign at the entrance. Even though the town is less than two hours away from Stockholm the catchphrase has stuck, possibly because there is only one road to Trosa, and those who drive it have to drive the same way out (pp. 268–269).

A lighthouse on the island of Öja in the southern Stockholm archipelago. A pilot station was founded here as early as 1535, and the lighthouse erected in 1651 was the first on Sweden's East Coast. In the early 1900s there were 120 residents on Öja, most of them pilots, lighthouse keepers and fishermen. Today there are about 40 year-round residents, most of whom work for the Swedish Maritime Administration. A sea rescue school operates on the island, and visitors can sleep overnight in the pilot's observatory while attending conferences (previous pages).

Tour skaters on the Nämdö channel in Stockholm's southern archipelago. This winter sport has become one of Sweden's most popular since its invention by the athlete Victor Balck a century ago. The long skate blades make it easy to build up speed, and if conditions are just right, with smooth, snow-free ice, a good skater can cover two hundred kilometres in a day.

Some of the names along the coast can pique the imagination. This reef and its lighthouse in the Stockholm archipelago are called Franska stenarna (the French Rocks). The name has nothing to do with France, but with a person or possibly a ship named on a 1691 sea chart as Frans Steen.

Stockholm's inner archipelago, otherwise known as Downtown, in the grip of winter. In the foreground is Beckholmen, with its aging docks and a huge crane receiving service. Behind that is the Gröna Lund amusement park.

Winter on a skerry called Långviksskär in the Stockholm archipelago. All the cabins are boarded up for the winter except Emmy Andersson's. The last permanent resident of Långviksskär, Emmy first got mains electricity in 2003 – at the age of 84 – through an eight-kilometre-long cable from a neighbouring island. Before that she had a windmill that generated enough power for a few lamps and a television (previous pages).

The Söderarm archipelago outside Stockholm just as the water is reaching the freezing point.

The sea at Vaxholm, an hour by boat from central Stockholm, is sluggish in the cold. Soon it will ice over.

Lygna archipelago north of Svenska högarna, with thin ice forming around the islets. One of the sheds on Lygna Hamn-skär, the largest of the islets, saved the lives of three Danish fishermen whose boat sank. After three days in a rubber raft, the three found protection from the elements in the shed and survived until picked up by the coast guard.

The *Waxholm II* en route from Vaxholm out into the archi-pelago. Many of the islands are served year-round by boat traffic. The operator, Waxholms-bolaget, runs nineteen vessels, including nine ice-going ships.

The fishing village of Rönnskär, close to the mainland at Stocka, north of Hudiksvall (previous pages).

The icebreaker *Oden*, the largest in the Maritime Administration's fleet, is a hundred and seven metres long and generates some twenty-four thousand horse-power. The *Oden* is normally stationed in the Bay of Bothnia, where ice often holds out until May and channels opened by icebreakers are vital to sea traffic for much of the year.

The Baltic Sea is still frozen when the West Coast starts to thaw. The sun is warm over the islands off Marstrand, and further out to sea the harbour seals are finding their way to the skerries to give birth to their cubs. And yet again, this characteristic landscape, where land meets sea, comes to life (overleaf).

PICTURE CREDITS

204 Hans Geijer, Naturbild
205 Claes Grundsten
206–207, 208, 209

Jeppe Wikström
NORTH COAST
210 Hans Strand
212–213 Roine Magnusson
214–215 Jan Töve
216 Hans Strand
219 Ove Källström, Norrlandia
220 L-G Abrahamsson,
Norrlandia
221 Jörgen Wiklund
222 Christer Häggström,
Norrlandia
223 Kjell Ljungström, Naturbild
224 Jörgen Wiklund
225 Jan Rietz, Nordic Photos
227, 228–229 Lars Bygdemark
230–231, 232, 233 Hans Strand
234–235 Claes Grundsten
236 Hans Strand
237 Jörgen Wiklund
238–239 Hans Strand
240, 241 Lars Bygdemark
242 Jörgen Wiklund
245 Lars Bygdemark
246–247 Klas Rune,
Naturfotograferna

WINTER COAST
248 Tore Hagman,
Naturfotograferna
250–251 Jan Töve
252, 254–255 Tore Hagman
256 Lars Bygdemark
258, 259 Håkan Sandbring,
Sydpol
261 Jan Töve
262–263 Håkan Sandbring,
Sydpol

265 Martin Borg
266 Hans Strand
267 Bengt Hedberg, Naturbild
268–269 Hans Strand
270–271 Jonas Forsberg,
Naturfotograferna
273 Claes Grundsten
274, 275 Jeppe Wikström
276–277 Malcolm Hanes
278, 279 Jeppe Wikström
280 Jeppe Wikström, Johnér
281 Magnus Rietz, Johnér
282–283 Hans Strand
285 Claes Grundsten
286–287 Jonas Forsberg,
Naturfotograferna

COASTAL LIVING

Around the Swedish coast lie 85 municipalities (kommuner) *which, each in its own way, safeguard and develop the sensitive coastal environment. Below is a sampling of some of the most active.*

BÅSTAD
www.bastad.se
Population: 14,200
Area: 218 km²

There is no big-city stress on Bjärehalvön: most homes are close to the sea, beaches, farms, meadows and golf courses. Building lots, homes and business parks are found just 10 to 20 minutes from Ängelholm Airport, but there are also bed & breakfast establishments, hotels and spas for the traveller seeking quiet relaxation.

Båstad is known for: The annual Swedish Open tennis tournament; Hallands Väderö nature reserve; Hovs Hallar, somewhat reminiscent of Spitsbergen and the Norrvikens Trädgårdar garden complex for all the senses.

Visitors to Förslöv can tour the Project Hallandsås exhibition covering the construction of a controversial 8.6 km railway tunnel.

———————————

HANINGE
www.haninge.se
Population: 73,500
Area: 458 km²

Haninge encompasses some 3,600 islands, islets and skerries. Here you will find bountiful nature, untouched forests and Tyresta National Park. At the same time, the municipality is home to two prestigious institutes of higher education: Södertörn University College and the KTH School of Technology and Health, affiliated with the Royal Swedish Academy of Sciences.

Haninge is known for: Dalarö, with its beautiful turn-of-the-century villas on the mainland and, off the coast, any number of ship-wrecks for divers to explore; the island of Kymmendö, where August Strindberg kept a writing cottage; Huvudskär, a small archipelago of seaward skerries and Utö, the most-visited island in the Stockholm archipelago.

Dalarö in Haninge is home port to the ketch Ariel, built in 1917 as a fishing boat and now a sailing training ship.

———————————

HAPARANDA
www.haparanda.se
Population: 10,200
Area: 927 km²

The Haparanda–Tornio area is the fastest growing region in northern Sweden and Finland, with a strong business climate including both trading and basic industry, as well as higher education and a well appointed residential environment. As a border city at the top of the Gulf of Bothnia, Haparanda is a hub for the arctic Baltic Shield and the Barents Sea region.

Haparanda is known for: A unique project with its Finnish twin city Tornio to create a common city centre where, for example, home furnishings giant Ikea has opened facilities.

Also found here is Sweden's only rail connection with Finland, continuing on to Russia.

———————————

HUDIKSVALL
www.hudiksvall.se
Population: 36,900
Area: 2,754 km²

With beautiful old farms, well-preserved fishing hamlets and the city's unique architecture, Hudiksvall combines a thriving cultural landmark with a strong focus on the future. The sea has always been central to the region's fortunes, and Hudiksvall harbour is currently undergoing an exciting transformation.

Hudiksvall is known for: Annual folk music gatherings

in Delsbo and Bjuråker; Optofiber – centre of the Fiber Optic Valley test facility. Since the 19th century, when sea traffic and timber trading were at their peak, the locals have been known as "Happy Hudiks" for their hospitality and friendly social life.

_____

HÄRNÖSAND

www.harnosand.se
Population: 25,000
Area: 1,064 km²

Founded in 1585 by King Johan III, Härnösand was built by merchants, tradesmen and craftsmen from throughout Ångermanland. Today, the city is characterised by a rich cultural life, a thriving economy and the charm of a small town. Stretching from the sea to extensive forested lands, Härnösand's urban landscape includes waterways right through the city centre.

Härnösand is the seat of the Diocese of Härnösand, encompassing the counties Jämtland and Västernorrland, and is a residential and university town long known as the "Athens of the North".

Härnösand was the first city in Europe to install electrical street lighting – in 1886 – with 80 lamps powered by a local hydropower plant.

HÖGANÄS

www.hoganas.se
Population: 24,000
Area: 144 km²

The Kullabygden district of Skåne offers lifestyle choices for all tastes. Close to both sea and forest, Höganäs features urban culture and a short ride to the local airport. Businesses enjoy reasonably priced offices and real estate, as well as easy access to other European countries.

Höganäs is best known for: Ceramics, chiefly for the dark, salt-glazed Höganäs jars and pitchers; Kullaberg, among Sweden's most-visited nature reserves, was awarded three stars in the famous Guide Michelin; Krapperup Castle, dating back to the 13th century.

_____

KALIX

www.kalix.se
Population: 17,300
Area: 1,815 km²

Kalix is the hub of the Norrbotten coastal region. Local buses will take you to a golf course in summer or a ski slope in winter. Outside Kalix lies Huvön, with its beautiful cliffs, and the last outpost, Malören. On this fascinating island is the "Bottenviken Cathedral" chapel, built in 1769 and well worth a visit for anyone interested in unusual architecture.

Kalix is famous for the local whitefish roe – the best there is!

The Archipelago outside Kalix is the northernmost part of the Gulf of Bothnia. The many islands vary from forest landscape to barren rock and sandy beach.

_____

KRAMFORS

www.kramfors.se
Population: 19,700
Area: 1,703 km²

Situated on Höga kusten (the Hight Coast), listed as a UNESCO World Heritage Site. Kramfors boasts the greatest concentration of businesses in Västernorrland County, with an economic base focused on forestry and mechanical industry. The local Culture School, with a curriculum of music, dance and theatre, has been honoured as "Best in Sweden". The Ådalsbanan and Botniabanan rail lines run along the coast, and should you need to reach the rest of the world, the airport is just north of the city centre. If you have a little extra time, spectacular natural attractions are just around the corner.

Kramfors is known for the family-owned bakery Polar-bröd, surströmming (fermented Baltic herring) and any number of "accordion kings".

The world's strongest paper is manufactured in Kramfors.

KÄVLINGE
www.kavlinge.se
Population: 27,500
Area: 154 km²

The municipality of Kävlinge includes dramatic stretches of coast, fine golf courses and great fishing spots. Excellent communications, a thriving business community and a wide range of cultural attractions make Kävlinge appealing to families and businesses alike.

Kävlinge is known for: Its many ancient remains, including the Stone Age Gillhög passage tomb and Barsebäck nuclear power plant, closed since 2005.

The Kävlinge municipal coat of arms symbolises a railroad crossing. The partridge is the municipal bird.

LULEÅ
www.lulea.se
Population: 73,300
Area: 2,110 km² (incl. archipelago 4,928 km²; land expansion 2 km² per year)

Luleå, with its bountiful nature, exciting culture, lively trade and sporting traditions is a growing community. Luleå is summer and sun as well as winter and snow; big-city pulse

as well as small-town idyll. The city's latest pride is Kulturens hus (House of Culture), with a library, art gallery and concert halls. The top floor houses an unparalleled collection of music from the Norrbotten region. Other attractions include the open-air museum Hägnan and Teknikens hus (House of Technology).

Luleå is known for: Gammelstads Church Town, an early-15th century stone church surrounded by 424 wooden houses listed as a UNESCO World Heritage Site.

There are 742 islands in the Luleå archipelago, plus some one thousand islets and skerries. The archipelago is accessible most of the year; passenger ferries serve the islands in summertime, and, when winter ices are strong enough, roads are prepared across them for vehicle traffic.

MÖNSTERÅS
www.monsteras.se
Population: 13,100
Area: 598 km²

Mönsterås is a "green municipality", partly because of its status as an ecological community, where sustainable development issues are a central facet of local development, and partly for its diverse forests, waterways and

cultural history. Along the 150 km coastline with its 300 islands are the mouths of the Alsterån and Emån rivers. The peninsula of Oknö offers fine bathing, camping and fishing.

Mönsterås is known for: The ruins of the Kronobäck monastery from the late 1400s, where lepers, wounded knights and sick pilgrims where cared for by monks belonging to the Order of St. John. Also found here are the old Pataholm market town and Gabriel Ceramics at Timmernabben.

Summers in Mönsterås are among the sunniest and driest in Sweden.

MÖRBYLÅNGA
www.morbylanga.se
Population: 13,600
Area: 669 km²

Go bird watching at Ottenby, visit the characteristic villages or take a botanical excursion among the unique flowers of the barren Alvaret limestone plain. Although Öland is among Sweden's smallest counties, there are 14,000 registered ancient remains. For example, on the south end of the island is Eketorp Fortress and King Karl X Gustav's "Great Wall" that defined the royal hunting grounds. During the Stone and Iron Ages, Öland was an important Baltic Sea trading area, and still today it boasts a healthy climate for business.

Mörbylånga is known for: Most of southern Öland is listed as a UNESCO World Heritage Site as the Agricultural Landscape of Southern Öland.

Öland Bridge, built in 1972, is more than 6 kms in length. Before the bridge, car ferries plied the route from Färjestad on Öland to the mainland.

NORRTÄLJE
www.norrtalje.se
Population: 55,000
Area: 1,938 km²

Norrtälje was granted city status by King Gustav II Adolf in 1622. Although the city and much of the surrounding countryside was burned by the Russians in 1719, there are a number of older wooden buildings which, together with the Norrtälje River, give the town its charm and character. The archipelago's history is dominated by a seafaring tradition, and the museum in Älmsta provides a telling image of this epoch.

Norrtälje is known for: Penningby Castle and numerous ancient rune stones and a cottage used by artist and author Albert Engström (1869–1940). The population of Norrtälje

has grown by 20 per cent in the last decade. The municipality encompasses no less than 54 nature reserves.

NYKÖPING
www.nykoping.se
www.boinykoping.nu
Population: 50,400
Area: 1,428 km²

Take a deep breath. Like the idea of a sea breeze, a simpler life and wide horizons? Nyköping is growing and turning towards the water. The coast pulls. Take time off on a Friday and paddle or sail out to your very own bathing rock on one of the Nyköping archipelago's one thousand islands. Then take a weekend trip to Paris or Berlin and drop your bag at home 15 minutes after landing. Find a new way of living an hour south of Stockholm.

Nyköping is known for: Spiced aquavit and untouched nature.

There are flights to more than 40 destinations from Stockholm Skavsta Airport, just outside Nyköping.

NYNÄSHAMN
www.nynashamn.se
Population: 25,100
Area: 357 km²

Everyone in Nynäshamn lives within ten kilometres of the

coast, and there is still plenty of small-town charm here – imagine walking down to your boat slip right downtown. Nearby villages like Ösmo, Sorunda and Stora Vika are surrounded by rolling farmland, while Stockholm is only 40 km away.

Nynäshamn is known for: The island of Öja/Landsort, which marks the southern boundary of the Stockholm archipelago.

Did you know? Nynäshamn is the sunniest spot in Stockholm County.

ORUST
www.orust.se
Population: 15,300
Area: 388 km²

The natural attractions of Orust vary from mighty sea to thriving farms, expansive forests and glittering lakes. Orust has always been associated with the sea, and enjoys an ancient boat-building tradition. A substantial portion of all the pleasure boats made in Sweden come from Orust. The well-known islands of Malö and Flatö are within the municipal boundaries, while far to the west, in the Bohuslän archipelago, lie the car-free islands of Käringön, Gullholmen and Härmanö which, together with Mollösund, are perfect examples of west-coast fishing hamlets.

Orust is known for: Käringön, Mollösund, Hälleviksstrand, Gullholmen and other living picture postcards.

Orust is Sweden's third-largest island and the largest on the west coast.

PITEÅ
www.pitea.se
Population: 41,000
Area: 3,112 km²

Winter darkness inspires the locals in Piteå to create and renew just as much as summer's round-the-clock sunshine. Here you will find great entertainment as well as peace and quiet, with unspoiled nature just around the corner. Piteå is your home away from home.

Piteå is known for: Pite Havsbad, the seafront camping and conference centre called the "Riviera of the North" and a city centre surrounded by water.

There are 530 kilometres of seafront on the mainland and islands within the municipality.

SKURUP
www.skurup.se
Population: 14,700
Area: 195 km²

Skurup is one of Skåne's new high-growth communities, surrounded by sea and high ridges, castles, farms and wide-open vistas. There is fine bathing beaches, beautiful nature, great sightseeing and a wide choice of leisure activities.

Skurup is known for: Selma Lagerlöf, one of Sweden's most-read authors, and her fictional, geography-loving character Nils Holgersson and Skurup residential college, with its renowned music and media programmes.

On the Swedish National Day in 2007, a new public monument was inaugurated: a 700-kilo, 15-metre high statue of Nils Holgersson riding on his goose. The bird has a wingspan of nearly eight metres.

STENUNGSUND
www.stenungsund.se
Population: 23,300
Area: 254 km²

When bathing resorts were all the rage during the 19th century, this was the gathering place of wealthy city dwellers, but today Stenungsund offers much more than a fine place to swim. The local Kulturhuset (House of Culture) is the focal point for arts. Svartedalen offers untouched nature for mushroom and berry picking, skiing and fishing. Stenungsund welcomes visitors with some 60 shops located right along the waterfront.

Stenungsund is known for: Its role as the centre of Sweden's petrochemical industry.

One of the world's largest regattas, Tjörn Runt, is held in Stenungsund each August with nearly one thousand participants.

STOCKHOLM
www.stockholm.se
Population: 788,200
Area: 188 km²

Stockholm is a city of contrasts – water and land, past and future, small town and big city, short winter days and sunny summer evenings. Stockholm is Sweden's capital and largest city, where municipal service companies employ nearly 50,000 people to keep daily life functioning smoothly.

Stockholm is known for: The Royal Palace in the Old Town; the enormous golf-ball-shaped Globen Arena; the museum housing the almost fully intact 64-gun man-of-war Vasa that sank on her maiden voyage in 1628.
Stockholm was granted city status around 1250. Nearly one third of today's Old Town is built "on water". The waterways separating the city districts are cause for the epithet "Venice of the North".

STRÖMSTAD

www.stromstad.se
Population: 11,600
Area: 471 km²

Strömstad's long history includes fishing and quarrying, and tourists have been drawn by the salty sea and resort life for decades. The local economy thrives on tourism and trade with neighbouring Norway, and on the specialised competence of many local companies.

Strömstad is known for: The Svinesund Bridge linking Sweden and Norway; Koster, Sweden's westernmost islands with a year-round population; the beautiful Bohus granite.

The municipal coat of arms symbolises a square-rigged lobster cog, the type of ship used to export local seafood to Holland and the rest of Europe in the 17th and 18th centuries.

SÖDERHAMN

www.soderhamn.se
Population: 26,200
Area: 1,065 km²

Söderhamn offers genuine small-town charm, with turn-of-the-century wooden houses. But the surrounding municipality consists of many picturesque villages and hamlets. At Norrala royal farm, King Gustav Vasa appealed to the Hälsingland farmers for help in a war with Denmark. In recent decades, the economic base has shifted from large-scale forestry to small and medium-sized companies in a variety of industries.

Söderhamn is known for: Skärså fishing hamlet and the old fishermen's district of Öster.

The Swedish forest products industry was born in Bergvik. The world's first sulphite factory was founded here in 1874.

SÖLVESBORG

www.solvesborg.se
Population: 16,700
Area: 186 km²

Sölvesborg features the finest sand beaches in Blekinge county, a charming town centre dating back to medieval times, fantastic nature for hiking and cycling, picturesque fishing hamlets and the scent of smokehouses. The local economy is characterised by positive entrepreneurship.

Sölvesborg is known for: Fishing hamlets on Listerlandet; the storied island of Hanö; expansive beech forests in Ryssberget.

You can fish in the sea or Grundsjön Lake on the boundary between Skåne and Blekinge. A specially built pier here offers handicap access.

TJÖRN

www.tjorn.se
Population: 14,900
Area: 168 km²

Tjörn's varied nature is a Sweden in miniature, with salt-water bathing, hiking trails, bicycle paths and bridges. Local history stretches back to the Stone Age, while the community of today lives in the present with a strong and growing economy with successful companies within the crafts, culture and tourism sectors. The population of Tjörn triples during the summer.
Tjörn is known for: The Sundsby säteri estate, dating from the 12th century, which opened to the public in 2003; the Pater Noster lighthouse, re-opened in 2007.

Tjörn hosts Scandinavia's only water-colour museum, with exhibits by international artists.

TRELLEBORG

www.trelleborg.se
Population: 40,500
Area: 342 km²

Together with the fertile lands of Söderslätt, sea and shore have always been Trelleborg's raison d'être. People come here to live and work, fish and bathe, or just be. In the Middle Ages, tradesmen came here for the herring so much in demand by the guilds of the Hanseatic League. Ships and cogs of that age have been replaced by modern car ferries serving German and Polish ports.

Trelleborg is known for: Smyge-huk, Sweden's southernmost cape, visited each year by hund-reds of thousands of tourists.

In 1714, King Karl XII landed at Stavstensudde.

VARBERG
www.varberg.se
Population: 55,900
Area: 874 km²

Take a deep breath and enjoy the breeze off the sea. You are sur-rounded by calm and the joy of life. Even the local economy is marked by a sound vision of the future. Varberg is a spa and resort town dating back to the 19th cent-ury. King Oscar II, Verner von Heidenstam and Gustav Fröding are famous Swedes who discovered Varberg early.

Varberg is known for: Its medieval fortress, promenade and a bath house built in 1903.

The Grimeton radio tower, built in 1924 to open a telegraph link to the United States, was a crucial World War II communication channel. It is now listed as a UNESCO World Heritage Site.

VÄSTERVIK
www.vastervik.se
Population: 36,400
Area: 1,881 km²

Outside the seventy-kilometre coastline are over 5,000 islands offering plenty of beauty and activities. To enjoy the privacy of your own bay is as peaceful as to linger in the periphery of the archipelago with blue seas as far as you can see. There is plenty of opportunity for privacy as well as for company. Several islands (for example Idö, Hasselö, Rågö and Sladö) offer a variety of services such as communications, restaurants, accommodation, guest harbours and activities.

Västervik is known for: The narrow gauge railway between Västervik and Hultsfred from 1879 with a daily service during the summer.

The listed boatman's cottages in central Västervik were converted to housing for the Crown's boatmen. Six of these are rented by the day or week.

YSTAD
www.ystad.se
Population: 27,600
Area: 352 km²

No city in Scandinavia, and few in the world, offers a more complete picture of days gone by than Ystad, with its more than 300 half-timbered houses. But this historical site is very much alive. Ystad is close to the world beyond Sweden's borders, with direct trains to Copenhagen and a growing international harbour. Ystad prides itself in being a great place to live and work.

Ystad is known for: Some 40 km of sand beaches; the Sand-hammaren lighthouse. Ales stenar, a megalithic monument dating from the end of the Nordic Iron Age.

Kurt Wallander, protagonist of novelist Henning Mankell's series of police thrillers, works for the Ystad police department. The books attract many "Wallander Tourists" to Ystad every year.

ÖCKERÖ
www.ockero.se
Population: 12,200
Area: 25 km²

The islands of Öckerö lie like a string of pearls between Vinga and Marstrand. Many visitors arrive by ferry or pleasure boat, and traffic in and out of the harbour can be heavy. Each island has its own character, with lively activity all year round. Inhabited islands within the municipal boundaries include Bohus-Björkö, Fotö, Grötö, Hyppeln, Hälsö, Hönö, Kalvsund, Källö-Knippla, Rörö and Öckerö.

Öckerö is known for: Fisheries, several shipyards, and, not least, the delectable Hönökaka soft bread.

Öckerö and Gotland are the only Swedish municipalities completely separated from the mainland. The Old Norse name for the area, Eikery, comes from the word for oak.

ÖSTHAMMAR
www.osthammar.se
Population: 21,400
Area: 1,471 km²

Östhammar is for those who like to keep a comfortable distance from the big city, but with cultural attractions nearby, rich opportunity for pleasant living and meaningful free-time activities, expansive nature and proximity to the sea. Here in Roslagen, sun worshippers can find just the right spot, fishers can expect a bite and wind surfers can be sure the wind will blow. Roslagen is inviting all year round.

Östhammar is known for: Vallonbruken, with its farms and parks; the Forsmark nuclear power plant and folk music events, including the Östhammar Music Festival.

Each January 13, the village of Gimo in Östhammar hosts the "knutmasso" carnival. The Knutmasso Museum explains the tradition all year round.

PICTURE INDEX

Almö 102–103
Alvaret, Öland 144, 145
Asperö 54–55

Baltic Sea 237
Barsebäck Golf 78
Bergkvara 113
Bergudden lighthouse, Holmön 242–243
Billudden, Uppsalaåsen 220
Biskopsö archipelago 209
Biskopsön 209
Bjuröklubb 244–245
Bjäre peninsula 64–65, 76–77, 87, 258
Björholmen 254–255
Björnö 190–191
Blå Jungfrun 129, 162–163
Bonden lighthouse, Norra Kvarken 224
Brantevik 94–95
Bredsand lighthouse, Gotska Sandön 160–161
Brofjorden 38–39
Bruddesta, Öland 151
Bråviken 117
Bullerö archipelago 286–287
Byrums raukar, Öland 140
Byske beach 227

Dämman lighthouse, Kalmarsund 128

Falsterbo 88–89
Falsterbo lighthouse 84
Falsterbo Strand 74
Falsterbokanalen 86
Fjällbacka 12, 23
Franska stenarna 274
Friseboda nature reserve 73, 98–99
Furusund 181
Fykan 252
Fårö 138–139, 141

Gaviksfjärden 238–239
Gillöga 168, 185
Gotland 136, 142, 143, 152–153, 154–157
Gotska Sandön 160–161
Gryt archipelago 104–105
Gulf of Bothnia 284–285
Gullholmen 40–41
Gävlebukten bay 220
Gothenburg 52–53, 256–257
Gothenburg archipelago 250–251

"Hahn's shacks", Öland 266
Hallands Väderö 69, 76–77
Hall-Hangvar nature reserve, Gotland 143
Hamburgön 248
Hanö 118–119
Hanöbukten bay 73, 83, 98–99, 118–119
Haparanda Sandskär 246–247
Haparanda archipelago 217, 246–247
Harstena 104–105
Helgumannen 138–139
Holmön 242–243
Hornslandet 233
Horsten 208
Hovs hallar 64–65, 258
Hudiksvall archipelago 232
Hunnebostrand 21
Hållö 18, 22
Härön 46–47
Hästvam 32–33
Höga kusten (High Coast) 236, 238–239
Höga kusten Bridge 212–213
Högbonden lighthouse 210
Hölickskär lighthouse 232

Ingarö 190–191
Ismanstorp hill fortress 149

Jordhamn, Öland 148
Jungfruskär 132–133
Jungfrusund 132–133

Kalmar Castle 125
Kalmarsund 128, 129, 165
Kalmarsund Park, Kalmar 124
Kalvesund, the canal 50–51
Karlskrona Maritime Museum 122–123
Karlskrona archipelago 120–121
Karlsö islands 158, 159
Kattegatt 76–77, 87
Koster islands 14–15, 28, 29
Kråkelund beacon 115
Kuggviksskären lighthouse 117
Kuggören 230–231
Kullaberg 70, 80–81
Kullen lighthouse 70
Kyrkesund, Tjörn 46–47
Kyrkviken, Möja 182
Kåseberga 92–93
Kåseberga harbour 259
Köpmanholmen, Yxlan 181

Lammskär 110
Landsort lighthouse, Öja 270–271
Lidingö 186–187
Listerby archipelago 102–103
Luleå oil harbour 241
Luleå archipelago 219
Lygna Hamnskär 280
Lygna archipelago 280
Lysekil 38–39
Långe Jan, Öland 166–167
Långsand 220
Långviksskär 178, 276–277

Malmö 85, 91
Marstrand 16–17, 286–287
Missjö archipelago 134–135
Misterhult archipelago 100, 130–131

Mollön 42–43
Morups Tånge 62–63
Måkläppen 69
Måseskär lighthouse 24
Möja 182, 198–199
Mölle 80–81

Nidingen, twin lighthouses
58–59
Norra Kvarken 224
Norrhamn, Vaxholm 172–173,
279
Norsten 205
Nämdö Channel 272–273
Närsholmen, Gotland 152–153
Näsudden, Gotland 156–157

Orust 40–41
Oskarshamn 126–127

Rakön 260
Ramsvikslandet 34–35
Ribersborgsbadet, Malmö 91
Rindö 173
Rivö 54–55
Ronneby archipelago 109
Rönnskär fishing hamlet 228–
229, 282–283
Rörö 250–251

Salsåker 214–215
Sandhammaren 66
Sandhamn 202–204
Sandhamnsleden sailing
channel 184
Sankt Anna archipelago 110,
114, 134–135
Sicklaön 186–187
Sigsarve beach, Gotland 143
Själsö fishing hamlet, Gotland
154–155
Skanör 90
Skomakarn, lighthouse 112
Skuleberget hill 234–235

Skuleskogen National Park 223,
234–235
Smögen 36
Sotenäset 34–35
Stenshuvud National Park 83,
96–97
Stockholm 275
Stockholm city archipelago 174
Stockholm inner archipelago 275
Stockholm archipelago 274,
276–278, 281
Stockholm south archipelago
270–273
Stockholm outer archipelago
286–287
Stora Alskär 194–195
Stora Fjäderägg lighthouse 222
Stumholmen, Karlskrona 122–
123
Sundre, Gotland 136
Sundsholmen 132–133
Sundsvall 225
Svangen lighthouse 37
Svenska Björn 176
Svenska Högarna 200–201
Söderarm lighthouse 196
Söderarm outer archipelago
170–171
Söderhamn archipelago 228–
229
Söderöra, Roslagen 188–189
Södra Väderöarna 31

Tjust archipelago 106, 112
Tjärven lighthouse 197
Tjörn 26, 46–47
Tjörn Bridge 44–45
Torekov 76–77, 87
Torne River outlet 240
Tosteberga 261
Trosa 268–269
Trosaån 268–269
Trässö 106
Turning Torso, Malmö 85

Ullångersfjärden 214–215
Ulvöhamn 216
Ulvön 216
Ursholmens lighthouse station 30
Utklippan 111, 120–121

Varberg fort and open air
swimming baths 56–57
Vaxholm 172–173, 279, 281
Ven 79
Vickleby, Öland 144
Vinga 27
Visby 147, 267
Vitemölla 60
Väcker, the lighthouse 48
Väderöbod, Södra Väder-
öarna 31

Ålandsskär 206–207
Åstol 19

Äleklinta, Öland 165, 262–263

Öja 270–271, 272
Öland 148, 149, 151, 162–163,
165–167, 262–266
Öland Bridge 164
Öresundsbron 82
Örskär lighthouse 179
Örö 130–131

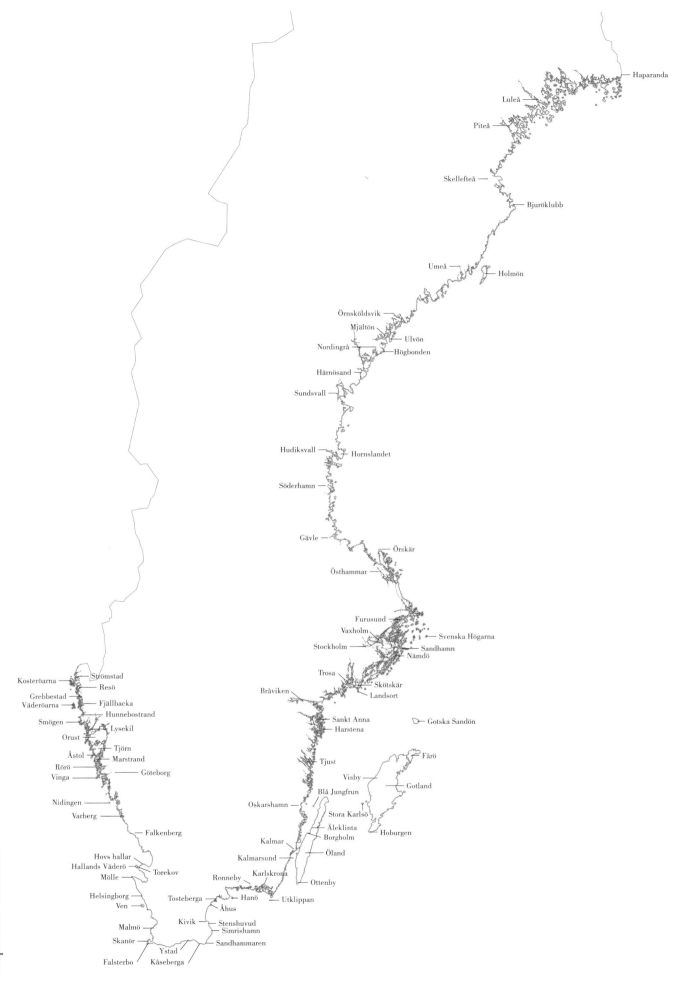

Haparanda

Luleå

Piteå

Skellefteå

Bjuröklubb

Umeå — Holmön

Örnsköldsvik
Mjältön
Nordingrå — Ulvön
Högbonden

Härnösand

Sundsvall

Hudiksvall — Hornslandet

Söderhamn

Gävle — Örskär

Östhammar

Furusund
Vaxholm — Svenska Högarna
Stockholm — Sandhamn
Nämdö

Trosa
Skötskär
Bråviken — Landsort

Sankt Anna
Harstena

Tjust — Fårö

Visby
Blå Jungfrun — Gotland
Oskarshamn
Stora Karlsö
Äleklinta
Kalmar — Borgholm
Hoburgen
Kalmarsund — Öland

Hovs hallar
Hallands Väderö — Torekov
Mölle
Ronneby — Karlskrona
Helsingborg — Tosteberga — Hanö — Ottenby
Ven — Åhus — Utklippan
Kivik — Stenshuvud
Malmö — Simrishamn
Skanör — Sandhammaren
Falsterbo — Ystad
Kåseberga

Kosteröarna — Strömstad
Resö
Grebbestad
Väderöarna — Fjällbacka
Hunnebostrand
Smögen — Lysekil
Orust
Åstol — Tjörn
Rörö — Marstrand
Vinga — Göteborg

Nidingen
Varberg
Falkenberg

Map: Martin Thelander